The Divine Human

Human

Starseeds, Soul Frequencies & Humanity's Cosmic Origins

Saira Salmon

ISBN: 9 798878 197861
Imprint: Independently published

Dedication

To Jeremy, with gratitude for the many times you have sat listening to me as I tried to make sense of things, and for all the help and support you have offered over the years.

Contents

Introduction -
We Are Not Who We Think We Are

You may have heard it said that humanity is a species with amnesia. What does it mean? And what are the implications of this for us as a race?

Not understanding our origins, or really any important part of our history and our beginnings, has huge implications as to how we understand ourselves, what we are capable of and manifesting our purpose as a race. It cannot help but impact every single individual negatively to be so badly disconnected from our roots.

Because if we don't know where we've come from how can we accurately and consciously plot our path forwards?

Currently Academia would have us believe that we all evolved from apes over several million years, until modern man began to emerge about 200,000 years ago. It's called the Theory of Evolution.

There's just one big problem with it – for over 150 years now they have been trying to find the facts to back up this theory without much luck. A few bits of fossil here and there, but no 'missing link' and various hypotheses are offered, none of which satisfy.

It's just a good story – in fact, not even that. Too many anomalies, too many unexplained physical objects that don't fit in with the theory, no matter how they try to shoehorn them. The best current approach to all of these anomalous objects that give the lie to the theory is to just.....ignore them.

Yes, really. If a physical artifact seems to give the lie to the current narrative it is ignored, overlooked, misplaced or ridiculed. Careers have been lost by those who refused to put on the blinkers and toe the line.

But these inconvenient artifacts won't go away, and more and more people are now beginning to question what we are told, and dig around for themselves to find some satisfactory answers that do make sense of the physical evidence.

And once you start to look it is surprising what you find – fossilised giants footprints are found all over the world, fossilised dinosaur and human footprints...together, old clay tablets with clear pictures of dinosaurs and humans together – all of which, according to modern history is impossible!

It goes on....ancient stone structures that predate by many thousands of years the supposed beginning of our history, areas of nuclear radiation as if from an ancient war – including a city where petrified human remains are radioactive, clearly man-made engineered objects found buried deep in ancient coal deposits.....

I've not even begun to scratch the surface, and it is a rich and mind-boggling area of research for those who wish to pursue it further.

What it clearly shows us, however, is that what we have been told would seem to have – at the very least – a big chunk of the story missing or – at worst – be totally wrong.

The question is why? Why would 'they' not tell us the truth? In trying to answer that we veer between cock-up and conspiracy theory.

Dig around long enough,

particularly in ancient lore and native legends and a different picture begins to emerge.

Once you become aware of humanity's cosmic origins and history you start to understand what has been going on here on Planet Earth for many, many thousands of years, and how the veil of amnesia has very deliberately been put in place to serve the hidden agendas of those who would – and do – rule us, dominate us, control us, use us, abuse us and enslave us as a race for their own purposes.

Sounds nuts doesn't it....but follow the trail of breadcrumbs with an open mind and in order to make sense of what you find you have to begin to re-arrange your concept of how the world is structured, and how much of what we are taught has been deliberately corrupted, re-written or mis-represented.

Why?

Well, that is quite a tale, the details of which are for another book. Here we are looking at who we *really* are, and the origins of the immortal soul we each possess, which is our true essence. We may have lost the memory of who we are, the sacredness of our lineage and the immortality for the physical body that was once our heritage, but the soul still knows its truths.

All we have to do is begin to peel away the layers to start to see the totality of who we really are, and the dazzling glory that is the potential that sits within each one of us. Our stolen legacy. As we begin to wake up from the long period of unconsciousness we have been put into we can begin to retrieve both our individual soul memories as well as our race memory and history.

Here, in this book I give you what I have found out so far about the innate gifts we each express in such a unique way, as well as the soul's point of origin as a Starseed birthed into this Time Matrix or universe.

Is it definitive?

No – we are just at the start of
rediscovering ourselves and I
have no doubt more
information will come through
as time progresses. But use this
as your starting point to reclaim
your place in the galactic
families we have been so
disastrously severed from.

12 Strand DNA

One of the important things to
understand about yourself is
that humanity's natural, organic DNA templating which forms the
blueprint for our physicality was a 12-strand template.

This means your 'blueprint' or DNA template was designed to be able to
carry 12th dimensional frequencies of sound and light codes.

That's very different to the 2-strands you have been told you have. And
most people on the planet are currently operating with only 2- 3 strands
of these 12 strands activated, and somewhere in the region of 95 – 98% of
their DNA capacity being inactive or what the scientists call 'junk DNA'.

It's not junk, it's been shut down. Deliberately.

And that is also a story for another time. But it is important to understand
this aspect of our soul origins and what it means to be a Starseed – you
have the potential to activate a minimum of a 12-strand DNA template,
with all that implies. Some have a 24-strand or even 48-strand heritage,
depending upon their lineage.

The 12-strand DNA template is called the Angelic Human template or
Diamond Sun DNA. There are other beings on this planet whose DNA only
has 9, 10 or 11 strands that they can activate and these are from the

Fallen Races, who eons ago deliberately changed their template in order to follow their own agenda – an agenda they are still following to this day, which includes the using, abusing and enslavement of other races for purposes of power and control and is proving so disastrous to humanity which is no longer even aware of the war which is being waged against it and its unique and precious DNA template.

I know many of you will have problems getting your head around this as you have been taught something very different. But please, hold this idea in your 'interesting but unproven' file until such time as you have gathered more information around what this means. There are plenty of other sources once you begin to look, with perhaps the most compelling being your own gnosis as you open you higher levels of information. Much of this information we can begin to access for ourselves once we are able to open ourselves to certain levels of frequency, enabling us, through our DNA, to begin to tap into a level called the Akashic, where individual and race memories are stored.

Many ancient, spiritual masters exhort us to 'go within' for our answers and to seek enlightenment, and they are reasons they ask us to do this, so we can KNOW from our own lived experience the spiritual truths that are withheld from us currently.

Fortunately there are many, many cosmic races, from multiple dimensions of our Time Matrix or Universe who are aware and who are helping us out of the mess we are in – they are called the Guardian Races who follow a service-to-others covenant called The Law of One[1].

You, incarnating here on this planet as a Starseed at this particular time is not a coincidence. Whilst there are many levels of aid and rescue missions aimed at this planet at this time, many beings from multiple star systems have been prepared to take on 'boots on the ground' missions in order to aid and advance the process of clearing thousands of years of

---

[1] See Appendix B

negative agendas and the amnesia they have caused, by those races whose fallen levels of consciousness seek to control and destroy others.

It is not a little thing to do – to come down into this very dense level of the Matrix, through the veils and the artificial memory-wiping NET[2] systems which cloak this planet, being born into physicality here without any memory of who you really are and why you are here, and inch by painful inch retrieving that understanding so you can start your mission.

The first part is waking up, and realising who you really are – a multi-dimensional being of light with a divine purpose, a member of the Christos family of races, with a potent and powerful purpose. Once you start to awaken and explore your Starseed origins and re-activate closed down areas of your DNA, opening yourself to other dimensions and a very different understanding of the nature of reality, things become really interesting!

Understanding the cosmic history of our Time Matrix which stretches back 950 billion years can help us to go through this process quicker, but requires an open mind and an open heart so you, yourself, can start to tap into your own individual soul memories as well as race memory on your own.

Our Universal God World 101

I have found it really helps to understand the Universe/God world/Time Matrix (insert any other word you might prefer) that we live within. This understanding helps us to locate ourselves within this Time Matrix, and gives us a clear understanding of our direct connections back to

---

[2] NET stands for Nibiru Electrostatic Transduction Field and is a frequency field anchored into the Earth and her grid systems which shroud the Earth with an interference pattern or electro-static force field preventing incoming and outgoing communication with the higher dimensional fields. It keeps Earth beings isolated from their natural connections to inner consciousness and spirit effectively creating a Prison Planet here on Earth.

Source/God/Universal Consciousness/All That Is/Creator (again, insert your preferred word for this concept – don't get hung up on semantics).

We are just one of many, many God Worlds or Universes that exist in the unimaginably vast fields of frequency and energy which surround and interpenetrate everything. Our Universe has been designed and brought into being as a 15-dimensional Time Matrix.

This means that there are 15 dimensional levels, from 1 – 15, that form the structure of this vast universe. Each dimension represents a frequency field, so you could just as easily say that there are 15 levels of frequency that make up this Time Matrix, with Dimension 1 being the lowest frequency and dimension 15 being the highest.

The illustration on the next page is a linear presentation of these dimensional levels which is easy to understand initially. As this understanding starts to bed in you will come to realise that in reality each density and dimension is really nested within the next – rather like Russian dolls, and relates to ever higher levels of sound and light frequencies.

The 15 dimensions are divided into 5 different Densities or what are called Harmonic Universes (HU), each of which describes different levels of consciousness and being:

> Harmonic Universe or Density 1 Dimensions 1, 2 and 3
> Harmonic Universe or Density 2 Dimensions 4, 5 and 6
> Harmonic Universe or Density 3 Dimensions 7, 8 and 9
> Harmonic Universe or Density 4 Dimensions 10, 11 and 12
> Harmonic Universe or Density 5 Dimensions 13, 14 and 15

It really helps if you can form some visual picture of this, as you begin to understand how vast both horizontally at the intergalactic level, and vertically at the multi-dimensional level just this one Time Matrix is.

It's enough to make your brain hurt – or at least, mine!

Most of humanity currently reside in the 3rd dimension, but more and more individuals, most of them Starseeds who are leading the way, are beginning to be able to consciously access other dimensions or levels of frequency as their DNA template begins to open up and activate in response to various energetic and stellar triggers.

We are at a time called a Stellar Activation Cycle[3]. It is a moment of potential for huge evolutionary change. A Stellar Activation Cycle happens approximately every 26,000 years. The sharp-eyed amongst you will immediately equate that to the Precession of the Equinoxes, or the time that our Earth's larger astronomical clock takes to complete a full transit around the plane of the ecliptic (the path of the sun in space as viewed from Earth) with regard to the fixed stars. This also equates to a complete cycle around the heavenly zodiac.

During a Stellar Activation Cycle for a period of years the universal interdimensional stargates open within the planet and there is the potential for the planet and everything on it to move our entire dimensional field up an octave into the next level of density or Harmonic Universe.

So there is a lot to play for but…. Our DNA coding provides the keys to both the planet and our own individual ability to pass through these stargates or frequency portals – it is the key that unlocks the lock. And in order to do this and move up into the next density we need to have *at least* 5 strands of DNA working, which means resonating at the frequency of the 5th dimensional field.

---

[3] This happens approximately every 26,000 years and is a period when the Universal Stargates on Earth open naturally and Earth and all her beings have a chance to move an entire dimensional field up an octave.

15 Dimensional Model Time Matrix Structure

Primary Sound Fields of Source Energy Matrix

HU 5	D.15	Blue Flame	3 Primary rays of sound and colour
	D.14	Gold Flame	
	D.13	Violet Flame	
HU4	D.12	Avatar Level	Entry point into densification of matter Pre-matter template
	D.11		
	D.10		
HU3	D.9	Oversoul (monadic) level	Etheric HU 3 home of 7D planet Gaia
	D.8		
	D.7		
Hu2	D.6	Soul level	Semi-Etheric HU 2 home of 5D planet Tara
	D.5		
	D.4		
HU1	D.3	Personality level	Full physicality HU 1 home of 3D planet Earth
	D.2		
	D.1		

This would not have been a problem if it hadn't been for the deliberate interference that has led to the shutting down of so much our DNA potentiality, as well as the hijacking of many of the stargate sites, by those hostile to the idea of wanting any form of spiritual evolution for the planet and her inhabitants.

As I said, a story for another time. Just remember that you source not just from within a small star system within – or in some cases without – our galaxy, the Milky Way. You also Source from higher dimensional systems that are waiting for humanity with its precious angelic DNA template to join them.

Starseeds from many cosmic worlds have answered the call for help from this planet at this time, and many are here, braving the rigours of incarnating into deep density, and the nasty, sticky web of amnesia, DNA tampering and deliberate sabotage, to enable the process of Ascension for as many of earth humanity as are willing to heed the call.

Not a job for the faint-hearted at all. So to every Starseed that is here, struggling to free us all from the sticky mess we find ourselves in I say thank you.

Thank you for your bravery, your caring and your compassion, for your showing up is not a little thing.

Part One -
Divine Soul Frequencies

1st Divine Soul Frequency	Divine Compassion
2nd Divine Soul Frequency	Divine Creation
3rd Divine Soul Frequency	Divine Order
4th Divine Soul Frequency	Divine Love
5th Divine Soul Frequency	Divine Self-Expression
6th Divine Soul Frequency	Divine Truth
7th Divine Soul Frequency	Divine Power
8th Divine Soul Frequency	Divine Wisdom

Soul Frequency
Introduction

At the top of our multidimensional Time Matrix consciousness exists as great Consciousness Collectives of sound and light. These are known as the Rishi, the Solar Rishi or sometimes the Breneau, and they are Founder consciousness.

They exist as great gestalts of consciousness in the form of spherical ante-matter constructs of thermoplastic radiation within the 3 primal light fields that form Harmonic Universe or Density 5.

These great Collectives of consciousness are themselves direct emanations of God/Source/ Consciousness/Creator into our Time Matrix.

It is from them that all Souls in this Time Matrix are brought into being. There are 8 major frequencies of energy that stream from them - a full octave – which resonates within each Soul. One of these frequencies usually expresses as the major frequency, whilst the others take a more minor role. Occasionally two frequencies share equal billing.

The point is, that whilst every soul, contains all these frequencies, one usually defines the way the Soul expresses itself in manifestation, and can therefore give us some insight into the natural and unique expression of that Soul and its innate gifts and talents and forms of self-expression.

This is the aspect of vital life energy in which we are most abundant and which gifts us with certain attributes which are an inherent part of our immortal soul, and we carry with us from incarnation to incarnation. Being able to align fully with these gifts in the way we live and work in the world brings us into flow and alignment with our divinity.

An integral part of any spiritual path is to know yourself – your True Self – and to express it coherently and authentically within Creation.

So learning of the most resonant frequency within a Soul can give us great insight into how congruent we are being at the level of the personality as well as helping us understand those often unappreciated aspects of who we are, that we may well take totally for granted and overlook they are so innate, but nevertheless can give us a great clue as to our Soul Mission.

Authentic expression, aligned to our Soul's frequencies and Natural Law is an important part of harmonious, balanced and integrated physicality. When we start to distort the energetic template by making choices against our Soul's innate expression we start to introduce dis-ease into our field and move from a state of balance to imbalance, with all the problems that brings.

There are 8 energy centres or frequencies that we are in resonance with to some degree, with the primary energy centre making up the dominant part of our Soul's frequency.

The first question anyone wants the answer to is 'Well, which am I'. If you are able to access the Akashic, and confident of your results, then you can find this information out for yourself. Otherwise, ask a practitioner to ensure you get correct feedback – someone not properly trained could well be tuning into the lower astral and being led astray by contact with some of the many negative beings there.

Remember, we all have all these frequencies within us, one is more dominant than the others thought – typically making up around 40+% of our expression, whilst the other between them make up the remainder.

So let's find out more about each frequency.

1st Divine Soul Frequency
Divine Compassion

Souls whose dominant energy centre or frequency is Divine Compassion are the caregivers of the world. They care deeply for people, community, plants and animals and all that comprises life.

They are all about compassion, community, nurture and nature.

A First Energy Centre Soul is highly compassionate, tolerant, concerned about family, society and planetary causes. They strongly resonate to the energy of the universal law 'All is One' and totally resonate with the fact that underneath superficial difference all of life is expressing the same Divine purpose.

When it comes to people they, least of all the energy centres, see no difference between race, colour, creed or any other 'differences' we use to justify separation.

Community therefore is very important to them – and this is one area that they excel in. If you are looking for someone to organise or create, structure or run anything community based, your First energy centre person will be totally committed and excellent in the role. And don't forget, community can mean anything from family, neighbourhood, school, a charity, volunteer work, on up to political, religious, spiritual-based or other groups.

First energy frequency souls are gifted with empathy and can use this gift in service to their community in a way which helps the community to thrive – social entrepreneurship and non-profit and community based enterprises are just a couple of the ways in which you see this gift being used.

They are grounded in helping others. What this means is that they are physically prepared to exert themselves to help others at a basic and practical level – getting shopping, helping with gardening, raising and nurturing children, cooking meals for the elderly, working in soup kitchens, teaching, social work, nursing, hospice care, growing food (sustainably, of course!), and working with environmental issues – anything from campaigning to boots-on-the-ground rescue work.

Any work that takes in this and contributes to the well-being of humanity at the level of basic human needs are areas where you will find the First Energy Centre soul. They find it both satisfying and their soul thrives when fulfilling this role.

It is important they feel a sense of belonging to some group, cause or community – this is when they feel and experience their Divinity, in relation to the whole, in its fullest expression.

Out of Balance
When we are not being fully authentic in our self-expression or get pulled into the negative polarity of our Energy Centre (and everything has a negative aspect!) then the shadow side of this frequency can start to be seen.

This energy frequency starts to slip into its negative when it becomes isolated. If these souls are not part of a community, or lose the sense of community in whatever way it may matter most to them, then they quickly lose their sense of Self.

Being alone, isolated or left out will pull them out of alignment very quickly and first energy centre souls need to address or eliminate situations where this occurs or take steps to change things.

This can potentially be at its worst when technically they are part of a group or community but feel isolated and left out of it. There is either the need to build bridges and mend this situation or walk away and find a more supportive community that is in tune with their aspirations.

It is hard, however, for a First frequency soul to walk away as they have such a strong need to belong, but they must find a place that fulfils their needs and rewards the efforts they put in. They need to not just contribute, but also to have their contribution valued and understood.

Just working harder in the hope they will be accepted and included will not necessarily change things. They need to find a group where they are valued and their gifts can shine. Otherwise they can come to feel somewhat bitter and frustrated, which to one with this soul frequency can be like a canker. It can also lead to coming from a place of neediness – needing to belong – and can be very disempowering.

Another aspect of imbalance is over-giving of themselves and their time which can badly drain their energy. Balanced Divine Compassion will always help others when they see need, but in such a way that does not undermine themselves, and helps to empower the Other wherever possible, and to build lasting resources wherever possible.

Remember, giving is part of a balanced flow of energy of giving and receiving. If they allow others to give to them, it will keep their well of Divine Compassion topped up so they can do the maximum good in the world – as well a role-modelling for others how to do this from strength and abundance, not need and inadequacy.

Very powerful indeed!

Dysfunctional
When this energy centre becomes truly dysfunctional it moves into sacrifice – it becomes highly other-focused, serving others in the effort to become valued and accepted. They see it as a strategy to move out of isolation, but in reality it depletes and leads them to a place of lack – lack of energy, lack of appreciation, lack of balance.

This Soul can end up becoming more and more depleted and trying to help from a place of lack, and identifying more and more with the people they are trying to serve to the detriment of their own healthy soul expression and experience. It can lead to creating for others and not themselves.

A dysfunctional First energy frequencies will justify this to themselves as being a selfish way to carry on. After all, they are not here for themselves, they will argue, but to serve. But being of service does not mean being a servant, and it is also a choice to serve, not a requirement and should be done from positive intent, not as part of a shadow play to make people feel indebted, or to make themselves feel better, or an ego need to ensure others know what 'good' people they are.

This energy centre can also use the strategy of 'taking on everyone else's stuff', over-empathising and participating in an effort to be 'part' of something. This mechanism can lead to over-compensation to the level where their own health, wellbeing and ability to help others can suffer.

Coming back into balance from a place of depletion – which is not unusual for those with this energy centre – can feel like being very selfish. They need to take time to attend to their own needs (which are different to wants and desires) before attending to those of others.

Healthy selfishness is about good boundaries and not developing a martyr complex!

It is important that they serve a community but not to their detriment and from a place of sacrifice – the community must return the value to them. They could do worse than remember the 'oxygen-mask' principle used on planes – put your own mask on before you help someone else. You are useless to anyone if you can't function.

Summary

1.   Strongly community based in their loyalties.
2.   Deeply committed to Life in all its forms.
3.   See beneath outer differences to the Divine within.

4. Empathic
5. Tolerant and committed to help making the world a better place.
6. Other focused – beware not to overdo it!
7. Need to feel a sense of belonging and involvement.
8. Need to be valued and understood.
9. Can become depleted when they lose sight of their own needs.
10. Isolation and neediness can lead to imbalance – find those who appreciate you!

Kuan Yin - Goddess of Compassion and Mercy

Kuan Yin is known as the Mother of Compassion and is revered as an embodiment of compassionate loving kindness. Her name means 'One who contemplates the sounds of the World' and it is said she hears the cries of all beings.

She vowed to remain within the earthly realms and help all beings until such time as all are liberated from the pain and suffering of the cycles of birth, death and rebirth.

Kuan Yin embodies the principle of Divine Compassion. Sometimes those with this energy centre can feel overwhelmed with the suffering and need in the world. When this happens call on this goddess and connect to her energy. She will nurture and sustain you, and guide you to bring your attention to where it can most help.

You cannot save everyone, but do what you can, and make that count and you will have done well.

2nd *Divine Soul Frequency*
Divine Creation

The energy centre or frequency of Divine Creation or Manifestation as it is sometimes called, is about bringing energies into form and is all about the joy of creation in, and experience of, the physical plane.

There are two major aspects to this energy – one is that of the physicality and sensuality of being here on Earth in a human body, and the second is the ability to manifest, to build, to create at all levels.

The energy of these souls should be focused on building and creating what is real, and tangible, and lasting.

Second frequency souls are gifted in creating almost anything. It can be a building something, creating a health and body awareness program, making a beautiful garden or even manifesting wealth or great relationships. All souls are creative, but Second energy frequency souls are particularly gifted in respect to bringing something through into matter – they can be great sculptors, for example, or builders or craftspeople or landscapers.

They get deep satisfaction from creating something that will stand the test of time – this is the energy of the creator, building, producing, creating something tangible and lasting at some level. It may be physical (as in building or designing a house), or it may be creating a business or enterprise of some kind, bringing in new technology or even creating some handiwork such as a beautiful piece of embroidery or a carpet, but it can also be intangible as in a brand or a vision of something new.

Whatever it is, it will always be something that has a place in the physical world.

This is also the energy that both teaches us about and celebrates the experience of being in a physical body. If dysfunctional conditioning and beliefs have not been introduced into them as children these are the souls who will know how to embrace it all – sexuality, money, the physical body, sensuality, adventure, the joy of life with all of its ups and downs.

They thrive on new experiences, especially those that are physical in nature. They are the people who travel the world exploring its physical surface and wild places - sometimes to the extreme! They love things like climbing Mount Everest, being athletic, doing yoga, going hiking or anything else which celebrates the physicality of the human body. They are the trendsetters who get us to experience our bodies in enjoyable and challenging ways.

So they enjoy physicality and using their body and senses – and this is true whether it be body-building, running, adventure sports, yoga, dance, gardening or even exploring new food and cooking ideas. They want to try it all and experience what a body is capable of. They are a role model for others as to how to be embodied and not just endure, but enjoy the experience.

They may or may not have great ease in acquiring money. If they embrace money as a physical creative energy they will attract it easily – that is unless they have societal or family overlays that get in the way of this. They may be drawn to study and work with money as the way the money system works fascinates them – finance, investing, banking and everything to do with building wealth.

Their ability to acquire it with ease will operate around their attitude to money. If they fall into the way of thinking that money is the be all and end all, it will not come with ease. However, if they recognise it as a creative energy and its importance in allowing them to enjoy life and all it has to offer it will flow with more ease.

Some can view this energy centre as being fixated on money, 'chasing' it, but this misunderstands how this energy centre perceives money – as a creative energy and one that can deliver new experiences not just in its creation, but in its use.

Money is important to Second energy frequency souls as it enables the full enjoyment of life and all it has to offer. It also enables them to give back to communities and help others, and if they have a healthy attitude towards the creation and use of money they can do good things in the world.

They can build success and abundance in their life by embracing and shaping the physical experience, and can manifest easily when in alignment with their divinity.

When they are aligned in this energy they will love creating new physical experiences, planning new things to try and experience, creating a business, manifesting wealth or creating something physical whether it is a beautiful garden, a piece of handiwork or a structure of some sort.

Out of Balance

When this energy centre starts to fall into imbalance and negative expression it will start to become ungrounded and disconnected from the physical experience of being alive.

Often, the Second frequency soul does not thrive at school in an academic environment, finding sitting at a desk and book learning tedious as they want to be out using their body – sport or something highly kinaesthetic is required.

Being in their head too much or focusing on intellectual pursuits and never getting out and moving their body physically will not help them thrive – either physically or from a success point of view. In fact being too sedentary is not good for either their mental or physical health. These are the people who might have a desk job but are out every weekend climbing mountains or biking long distances - they need this to stay balanced. Being 'in their head' is not good for them.

Financial abundance is tied to this physicality and becoming moribund, sedentary, in their head and desk bound, can lead to lack and their manifesting fire is damped down. If this happens it can become catch 22 as they can withdraw further into their heads to try and figure it out. Being in the physical body without money to create new experiences will not be enjoyable for them either – they need to move, run, dance or whatever calls them in order to get their juice back!

A lack of physical safety will also create disconnection from the physical realm and if there is this feeling it needs to be addressed.

Often those with this primary energy centre might incarnate into difficult or unpleasant experiences at the physical level. This can be through past negative choices that are being played out karmically or it can be a way of ensuring their soul experiences circumstances in this lifetime that can lead to great soul growth.

Dysfunctional

When it becomes dysfunctional this energy of Divine Manifestation or Creation can become highly ungrounded and disconnected from the physical. It then starts to seek excessive or potentially destructive physical or emotional sensations – getting high on drugs or alcohol, doing extreme sports or something similar, creating emotional dramas, or ramping up stress as it is the only way they can feel alive.

The Second Energy centre needs to get out of their heads and not get stuck in their inner world and begin to create outwardly. Emotions need to be released and not wallowed in, thrill-seeking - whether it is sky diving, over-eating, alcohol, drugs or even sexual addiction - needs to be seen for what it is. A poor substitute for tapping into the joy of being alive and experiencing all the wonders of the physicality of being alive in the third dimension.

Summary

1. Know how to bring energy into form.
2. Take great pleasure in the physical experience of life in all its forms.
3. Like to build, create, produce something of lasting value.
4. Thrive on new experiences
5. Can role model for others how to be fully embodied.
6. See money as a creative energy which enables them to experience life.
7. Need to fully embrace the physical experience in a healthy way.
8. Working or living a sedentary life or 'in their head' is highly unhealthy for them.

Mother Gaia

The Goddess Gaia was seen by the Greeks to be the primordial Creator of all life. From her sprang the starry heavens as well as the Earth and all its abundance, including all the other gods.

Gaia as the great Mother Goddess has been worshipped and acknowledged by humankind down through the Ages. As the embodiment of the creative principle she both initiates and destroys life. The great cycles and rhythms of the year and nature are her gifts to us, and remind us of the ever changing nature of being.

Often depicted as a pregnant woman she embodies fertile creativity. Those born with the primal frequency of Divine Creation can tune into her energy when they feel their own inner fire, inspiration and joy in life die down and there is danger of turning to destructive addictions to get the 'high' of being alive. Tuning into her and the abundant and rhythmic quality of her energy can help re-ignite that inner creative potential to experience life to the full, without becoming self-destructive.

3rd Divine Soul Frequency
Divine Order

Third energy centre souls are all about balance, harmony, beauty, art, law and order, perfection, peace. They bring order to chaos.

Fairness and peace are very important to them – whether it is creating a beautiful environment, a fair society or just keeping things in good order.

They are expert at being in balance and harmony with themselves and their environment and will work hard to make this happen – they may study Feng shui, or colour, become designers or architects, or even landscapers but whatever they do it will be with the aim to bring harmony and balance to a place, environment or situation.

Third Energy frequency souls have a wonderful aesthetic sense, and can be highly creative and artistic. They like to create in a way that respects beauty and harmony and doesn't upset the balance of things too much.

Third energy centre souls are the architects that know how to combine both form and functionality, and instill balance and harmony as well as blending beauty of form with great functionality – a real gift, as we have all experienced great looking products that are not really fit for function!

This is a great gift and not to be underestimated, and if they are drawn to this aspect of design they make great Product or Industrial Designers, Architects etc, who can produce items that fulfil their practical function but are also a joy to use.

They are nurtured by beauty and need to ensure that they have this around them, otherwise they can become depressed – environment is always important to those with this energetic frequency primary in them.

They also know how to present themselves well – know what works, what doesn't, how to combine colours and so on. As a result they make good stylists, interior designers or any profession that requires a good eye for what works.

There is also an innate sense of fairness and they really understand the balance of choice and consequences – the law of karma does not have to be explained to them, the concept is innately understood that you reap what you sow, and they can help others realise that nothing is without consequence, rights have responsibilities and everything you do has an effect.

Law and order are important – it might be that they chose to express this by joining the Police force, or by studying for the legal profession. They will uphold this structure of Law and Order if it is fair - otherwise they will be found fighting on the other side to bring in fairness and justice!

Third frequency souls love organised and harmonious systems – they are excellent planners and project managers, and love to bring structure and organisation to projects etc. This ability to establish order not only makes them very good planners and organisers, but they can help people to bring order and structure to the chaos of their lives as coaches, de-clutterers etc.

They find it easy to break things down into small chunks – a step-by-step approach that makes it easy for people to understand, learn and follow. They make excellent trainers and teachers in education and business as they can break down complex systems and methodologies into simple steps or bite-sized chunks.

When they feel organised, well-presented and well-prepared third frequency souls are happy to be the centre of attention and can take the spotlight in the world of public speaking or public presentation – but they need to feel 'together' for this. If they feel scattered or unprepared in any way, this will not work for them so it is important if they take on this role to always ensure they are properly prepared and to stay centred and balanced.

They make good leaders as they have a flair for organisation and efficiency – but only in those areas where this type of leadership is what is required. There are different kinds of leadership approaches for different situations. In a settled environment where the need is to build new and efficient systems for the future they will thrive.

Imbalance

The negative polarity of this energy centre is drama!

They hate drama and emotional scenes and upset – it oversets and shatters their balance. And this then leads to the imbalanced state of this frequency, as they will do almost *anything* to keep the peace – whatever it takes, no matter the cost to themselves!

This can lead to people-pleasing or inauthentic behaviour in order to re-establish calm. Rather than changing themselves to keep the peace, their strategy needs to be either to renegotiate what is happening or to eliminate the drama queen relationships from their life. (This means good boundaries and respecting their own needs!).

They also hate people being upset at them and again will try to accommodate others to keep in people's good books, which once again can lead to inauthentic behaviour.

Third energy centres can also fall into trying to manage everything and everyone around them in order to minimise drama and upsets in their life so it is essential they are careful about indulging controlling tendencies – they start to develop controlling tendencies in order to maintain order!

This is not only a waste of energy (and very annoying for others), but unrealistic as drama is inevitable at some stage in life, none of us avoid it, and if they come up with strategies to do so, it will result in inauthentic behaviour and also being quite controlling and managing.

So what needs to be addressed is the issue or situation causing the drama in the first place or, if this can't be done, to eliminate the situation/relationship causing the problem(s) by walking away. Otherwise their focus is going to be in the wrong place – trying to manage others rather than creating their own life experience!

And that is what the Third frequency souls are here to do – bring order and harmony to the world around them, not micromanage other people's lives or compromise their own.

Dysfunctional

The more they fall into imbalance, the more dysfunctional their energy will become – ending up with perfectionism and stagnation.

In order to prevent the drama of failure they will try to excessively organise and micromanage every little detail, and keep going over the same old thing rather than moving forwards or producing or doing much. Nothing ever gets completed because it is never quite perfect and so nothing gets achieved. It all goes through draft after draft, always with room for improvement, but never gets put into action.

Wanting everything to be perfect takes up a huge amount of energy and achieves little more than standing still, the status quo. The need to get everything right can lead to getting stuck. It can also lead to a huge sense of failure and disappointment because when their perfect plan or perfect life doesn't materialise it can be seen as a personal failure and there is the danger of becoming bitter about life generally.

There is also a word of warning that their love of beauty may also become an obsession with outward appearances and status and so on, stemming from a fear of being seen to be less than perfect, which brings in a layer of artificiality and lack of authenticity. If the focus is on how they think other people see them, or how they present themselves, it will paralyze them from moving forwards effectively and in alignment with their gifts and engaging in the positive expression of this energy.

Some can view a Third Energy frequency soul as quiet or reserved because of their tendency to do their work quietly and efficiently. The extreme shadow side of their gift can be in suppressing emotions which can lead to depression. They need to give themselves permission to make mistakes, and say that they are okay with that and it is not the end of the world!

It is important they remember that they are here to have an experience, and NOT to get it right every time.

Summary

1. Brings structure and order to chaos
2. Harmony at all levels is important, as is justice and fairness.
3. Highly refined aesthetic sense.
4. Architects of form and function.
5. Have a good sense of style.
6. Innate sense of fairness and understanding of cause and effect
7. Need healthy boundaries to keep balanced.
8. Good organisational leaders
9. Cannot bear drama and emotional upsets to the point they will compromise themselves.
10. Need to beware perfectionism and controlling behaviour.

Ma'at

The Egyptian goddess Ma'at personified truth, justice and cosmic order. It was she who oversaw the balancing of the heart of the deceased against the feather of Truth as she held the scales. But Ma'at represented more than this – she personified the Divine Order and Cosmic Order established at the beginning of Creation, which governs all life and takes in justice, truth, natural law, social order, political order and the right place and harmony of all Life.

When emotional upheavals or life's drama start to destroy the harmony those born with this primary frequency need, call on Ma'at to help you, and take time to tune into the vibration of cosmic order and harmony she represents.

4th Energy Centre
Divine Love

This is the frequency of Divine Love and Healing. Love is the vast creative consciousness and energy which permeates our Universe. Those with this primary energy centre are like the rays of the sun that reach out with healing warmth to envelop everyone.

People want to spend time around them, to be with them, because being around them feels good, and one always feels better for the experience of time spent in their presence.

Those whose Soul is born with this primary frequency are natural healers – it is an innate part of who they are as Love brings such a healing frequency with it. They may not necessarily work in the healing professions but they have a healing presence, and when around them others feel as if the broken pieces of themselves are coming together.

This energy centre is non-judgemental and is like balm to the soul as people feel loving acceptance around them. To be accepted for who we are, without judgement, is not something which is easily found and can be immensely soothing and healing to those who feel diminished by the judgements of others. Fourth energy frequency souls can hold a 'sacred space' for others, enabling them to reclaim the lost, misunderstood or even reviled parts of themselves.

As you can imagine then, if the Fourth energy frequency soul chooses to work within holistic health, this healing ability can be used to great effect, but even if this path is not chosen they will still be able to help those around them back to wholeness simply by being in alignment with who they are.......There is, of course, a proviso here which is that it requires them to be their authentic selves and not have erected facades and barriers, as can happen for many sensitive souls in this rather brutal world.

In reality it doesn't matter what profession this energy centre undertakes to be part of as long as they can be around people they can support and just radiate who they are.

It shouldn't have to be said, but it bears mentioning, that any support given is as part of a mutually nurturing relationship, otherwise it is out of balance and not a fair energy exchange. As we know, there are many takers in the world who are all too happy to take whatever is offered without giving and the Fourth energy centre if it is not wise to this can find themselves very drained by those who have no intention of a fair exchange.

The energy of Divine Love enjoys being with people. Others trust them and will have a tendency to share things easily with them, opening up to share concerns and problems that they might not talk about easily to others. They are excellent listeners and people feel heard and seen by the Fourth energy frequency soul, and not judged or thought less of, whatever their issues are. As I said before, they can be balm to a wounded soul.

They are generally very giving of their time and attention, being deeply caring souls, but need to beware becoming a well-used doormat by those unscrupulous or needy enough to not respect this generosity. It can be one of this energy centre's biggest learnings as they often struggle to establish healthy boundaries. It is vital to understand that looking after themselves, as well as others, is an essential part of the compact. If someone takes and takes, with no reciprocity in any form it is essential to be firm and enforce healthy boundaries - in a loving and gentle way, of course - as the Fourth frequency soul's kindness can easily be taken advantage of to their detriment.

Whilst caring and looking after others is a wonderful thing, this must never be at the expense of the Self. Love is the strongest power in the Universe, but here on Earth it is not a bottomless fountain. It needs replenishing and nurturing and appreciating and honouring in turn. These are souls who should be highly regarded and respected, not used by those too selfish to care.

Not surprisingly, this primal frequency is good at relationships, and always sees the good in others. Lovely a trait as this is – and it is! - it can sometimes lead to being disappointed. Relationships here on Earth are still very transactional, and although this might not be the way the Fourth energy frequency approaches things there are certainly others who do, so they may well find themselves feeling very let down or disappointed if a partner/friend/co-worker/family does not live up to their better side. The Fourth energy centre are forgiving souls, but this does not prevent the hurt and the pain this can sometimes cause.

They need relationships – this primal frequency is not a lone wolf – and loving and taking care of others and being taken care of in turn is very important to them. But, at the risk of repeating myself, it must be in balance – nurturing and being nurtured, not a one way street, but a proper exchange of energy. It is easy to fall into imbalance if they are not careful and then they end up very drained and are of no use to anyone - hence the need for good boundaries!

One of the major contributions this energy centre can make is to role model how giving and receiving can work to the benefit of all – when working in a healthy way the flow of love and non-judgement works in both directions and can demonstrate another way of being and living in the world for those used to only seeing taking, taking, taking.

This energy centre makes excellent team leaders as they make their teams feel appreciated and taken care of, held and supported, providing a safe space in which people feel encouraged to stretch into their full potential, and this generally brings the best out in them. People are very loyal to those souls with this energy frequency as they evoke this quality in others.

Their gifts will help them excel in any environment where people need to feel nurtured and cared for – healthcare, customer services, hospitality, or the numerous other people-centred professions.

Another aspect that can come in with the frequency of Divine Love is naiveté. It can involve wishful thinking and not wanting to believe some people really do choose to do bad things. The desire to see the best in people can be taken to the extreme, because to face an unpalatable truth will mean they have to confront things which are not pleasant.

This level of denial, if not addressed, can lead to big problems further down the line. Divine Love does not mean entering into a fantasy of unicorns and rainbows. Divine Love is tough, it is strong and it can look reality in the face, and still shine through. It loves *despite* the faults, not because of a blindness to them.

We live in a Universe of polarity – there is Dark as well as Light and Divine Love knows the Darkness but chooses the Light (whilst holding compassion for those stuck in the dark).

In a balanced loving state this energy frequency does not deny the shadow in others, it chooses to see the reality of what is before it …… and love anyway, but it is also realistic when it comes to trust. It is not a case of trusting others to be who we want them to be, but trusting them to act in coherence with their nature. It takes clear vision and insight to see the truth of others, and the energy of Divine Love can do this....and still shine the Light of Love on these individuals.

A healthy Fourth energy frequency soul will not, however, be so naïve as to put themselves into a position where they might be betrayed and duped when a bad'un acts in full accord with their fallen nature.

Imbalance

The negative polarity of the Fourth energy frequency is lack of support. When they are not receiving this and allow the situation to continue unaddressed it can set in motion a slow slide into dysfunction.

The worst thing for this centre is when they feel they are going it alone, shouldering all the burden and are not being nurtured or supported or appreciated by those around them. If this is the case they must either address the situation quickly or eliminate the cause from their life otherwise this will lead them into a dysfunctional relationship with their gifts and talents. They will probably find this hard to do, and come up with many excuses for others poor behaviour, but if they do not take action not only will they end up feeling abused, taken advantage of and unsupported, but this will drain the wonderful gifts they have to bring to the world.

Learning to say no, to be conditional with those around them is a lesson this energy freuqency has to learn. They have to become discerning about striking a balance with others between giving and receiving. They have to learn a healthy selfishness so they can function in the world as they are designed to do - it is not selfish to expect support and something back. In fact, this free flow of energy is fundamental to healthy living and abundance for all. This energy centre finds it so easy to give, they must be equally open to receiving and ensure this channel keeps open.

When someone is taking more than they give, Fourth energy centre souls will tend to go into a behaviour pattern of 'modelling' to the other what it is they want to receive in the hope that they get the message – rather than just sitting them down and telling them. So if they want a little care and nurturing, they will lavish this on the other – showing them what it is they want. Their somewhat faulty thinking is that if they give and demonstrate what it is they are wanting to get, then the other person will reflect this back to them. This is far too subtle for most people who will just take – and hopefully appreciate – the attention they are receiving, little realising this is meant to trigger them into like action!

Not surprisingly, the desired outcome rarely happens, others rarely respond in the way fourth energy frequency souls hope – they just keep on taking! If this situation isn't addressed by sitting down and talking clearly about what support is needed/expected this energy centre will become frustrated and resentful, tired and depleted.

Problems can also arise when they begin giving to others without them asking for their help. This can be done with the best of intent, but usually elicits little in the way of thanks or acknowledgment or even any gratitude. What Fourth frequency souls need to remember is that they can and should allow others to fix themselves first and only step in with help if asked – especially if their advice is not appreciated! The archetype of the rescuer is a dysfunctional aspect of this frequency, and can be very disempowering to others, even though it may be done with the best of intent.

Dysfunctional

If this behaviour pattern becomes entrenched, maybe through a desire to do good, or be seen to do good, it can fall into the dysfunctional aspect of this energy which is the martyr complex – someone who gives without receiving back and presents themselves as long suffering.

It is both co-dependent and abusive and does not respect the immense gifts of this energy centre or allow them to shine in any way.

Not surprisingly few people appreciate living with a martyr and being put on a continual guilt trip, so it can lead to trouble, which compounds the problem!

There can be a tendency also to act all helpless, like a baby bird, which is demeaning to them and out of integrity with their energy. The imbalance has become dysfunctional to the extent that instead of seeking mutual support and nurture they will want someone to take care of them and handle life for them – it is very childish and disempowered.

Responsibility will be abdicated for finances, aspects of business and life decisions and so on as someone else is required to take responsibility for their life. In addition, blame will be passed on when life does not go the way they want it too, no responsibility will be personally taken. It is very immature and toxic.

This can then lead to a sense of victimisation as they feel the world is an unfair place, taking the martyred stand that they give and give and never get back.

It is imperative this energy frequency gets the balance right between giving and receiving even if this means making some big changes in how they have chosen to structure their life. It means growing up, and treating others as partners, equals and expecting that everyone – including themselves – will take responsibility for their life and actions.

Summary

1. Their presence is attractive and healing to others.
2. Very healing and loving energy, balm to a wounded soul.
3. Non-judgemental energy which makes others feel accepted for who they are.
4. Can role model healthy giving and receiving.
5. Easy to talk to and confide in.
6. Good at relationships and need others in their life to thrive.
7. Make good team leaders.
8. Need to learn to say no and have healthy boundaries otherwise can become a doormat.
9. Need to be upfront about their needs to others.
10. Can fall into rescuer energy if they are not respectful in how they offer help.

Hathor

The Egyptian goddess Hathor is a goddess of love. She is often likened to the Greek goddess of romantic love, Aphrodite, but Hathor encompasses not just love in all its forms, but beauty, pleasure, music and so much that brings joy in life. She was a powerful ancient Mother Goddess, and was said to be the consort of various powerful gods and mother to their sons.

As the Eye of Ra, she was protective – like a mother lioness guarding her young – and whilst loving, could be fierce in protection of that love. She was sovereign unto herself, what she gave she gave freely, and she beautifully epitomised the balance between love of Self and love of others.

When you feel put upon, taken for granted or under-appreciated, tune into this beautiful loving, sovereign energy and call upon her to help you remember the love you have for all, whilst not being taken for granted.

5th Divine Soul Frequency
Divine Self-Expression

This energy frequency is all about self-expression, communication and speaking with one's own authentic voice.

It is the realm of the spoken and written word – many with this energy centre become wordsmiths (writers, journalists, playwrights) and actors, orators, communicators.

These Souls are the great communicators among us. They share their gifts through the use of language whether it be written or the spoken word, and possess the great gift of being able to inspire other through the use of words.

Language is important to them and they will have a relationship with language others don't – it will have taste, texture and substance for them. Words matter and Fifth energy frequency souls instinctively understand this. Words can create someone's reality, can cast a spell. They have power, and finding the right words matters – this energy centre knows this and knows how to use words carefully.

They know how to inspire people through words, how to help people see and understand new concepts and ideas by framing things in such a way that they paint the right pictures with words to communicate the essence of what they are sharing.

They can use this gift to help others change their way of seeing and thinking about things and introduce new ways of looking at life.

At this time, where technology and online media has simplified the process of getting a message out to a global audience, the fifth energy centre soul who knows what they want to say can quickly access millions of people with a powerful voice and gather a group of like-minded individuals together.

Often what holds a fifth energy centre back is not being clear about what their message is, what they want to share or communicate. So this can be where the work needs to be done, by establishing what lights them up at a soul level, so they can inspire others in a similar vein.

Many with this gift are drawn to publishing their original thoughts or to sharing what they know with others through public speaking, writing or even social media. It is important that this energy frequency shares and teaches the truths that it has arrived at, their unique point of view, not rehashes someone else's wisdom.

The Fifth energy frequency soul is highly verbal – they can be constantly talking and teaching in the way they talk, even to the level of conversing with themselves. There can also be lots of mind chatter if they don't have others to share with!

They will want to 'talk things through' and for someone to listen to them whilst them work things out verbally for themselves. They don't easily resolve things 'in their head' but need to talk it out loud. They therefore need to ensure they find friends who are willing to help with this, otherwise they won't get the clarity they need easily.

It is not unusual for them to blurt out golden nuggets of information when talking to others. There can be a natural gift of channelling in the moment when there is an audience and they are in the flow of energy and can find themselves spontaneously accessing an inner wisdom which often surprises even them! They are a natural channel, but this cannot be forced, it happens in the moment. So they need to pay attention when they hear themselves speaking words of wisdom that seem to come through them rather than from them!

It is important that this energy frequency uses words in some way to make a living – whether it be speaking or writing. There are lots of options in this respect, not just the obvious forms of writers etc. They can be very good marketeers and sales people, using words to persuade, or any other area of business where good communication skills are important – politics, diplomacy, advocacy, law for example.

They can also be excellent teachers either within the education system or some other learning modality, as trainers or lecturers or presenters maybe, but often like to settle in as a lifelong students and learners.

They can be prolific content creators, but it is important that this energy centres uses its own learning and experience to produce something unique to them – this must be their work, not a rehashing of someone else's. Anything else is just plagiarism, and whilst they might have some success at this – they are Fifth energy frequency after all, they know how to use words – unless they honour their authentic voice and truth, they are not accessing the full potential of their gift. It is important that they are aware of and avoid this trap. Of course, they will learn from others but what they create needs to be their own unique synthesis of the wisdom and learning they have acquired. It should be unique to them and their own lived experience to be original content.

Authenticity is important to this frequency – and this should show up in all they do. Which means they need to work out what authentic is for them! What does that mean? What do they stand for, what are their values, what is important to them, what do they like/dislike?

It is important to express their own unique opinion and expertise, gathered from their own experience and results. They have strong opinions and are not afraid to speak up but should ensure these are their views and not someone else's – they can get on a soapbox here and will come unstuck if they are not being congruent with who they are and what they truly believe. Their gift is not being honoured if they are parroting other people's opinions.

Finding an audience for what they have to say and share is important. This group can sometimes become outspoken or have a tendency to "talk,

talk, talk", because the written and spoken word is so important to them, and if they don't find a willing audience for their brilliance they are likely to become very frustrated.

Imbalance

Every energy frequency potentially has a dysfunctional side and the Fifth energy frequency starts to fall into imbalance if they do not have an audience. They must have someone to hear them – they need willing listeners!

Without this the power of this energy centre is wasted – someone has to hear them, they have to interact with someone. So it is important fifth energy centre souls find an audience who wants to hear and share what they have to say, not remain stuck in a library, studying, learning and writing for just themselves.

Otherwise there is the danger that, desperate to be heard, they will become inauthentic in what they say in order to appeal to those immediately around them, looking for the populist message and saying what they think people want to hear, in order to get the audience they need. They will adjust their message to ensure they find someone to listen to it, rather than honour the truths they have arrived at.

This increases the danger of plagiarism as they try to copy a message they see people are responding to or having success with. It can be a great temptation to see where the audience currently is, and then give them the message they want to hear. They have to find their own message as their real success – and satisfaction - lies this way.

Anything else is dishonouring the power of their gift.

Dysfunctional

The Fifth energy frequency also needs to be aware that not everyone wants unwanted advice or information no matter how well intentioned – it can be really inappropriate and is a dysfunctional aspect of this frequency when it offers information (or lectures!) where it has not been requested.

They also have to beware of talking for the sake of it! It is entirely possible they can come to like the sound of their own voice, but it dissipates the magnetism of what they have to offer if it is just blah, blah, blah.

Another potential pitfall can be to become what is called a Spellcaster, where they use words deliberately to weave a net of deception or illusion. Every good trickster or fraudster does this, and with the help of the Fifth energy centre behind them they can be very convincing. Needless to say, this is an abuse of this gift.

A Fifth energy frequency soul without an audience over the long term can become very dysfunctional in that they can retreat into the spiritual realm, or a make-believe world where, in their imagination, they find the audience they require, and are listened to. Or they may also journal endlessly day after day, to no great effect, finding an outlet in their journal, but never sharing their insights and message with an audience, wasting their gift.

They need to serve the world through the great gifts of communication they have and not hoard their words and messages, the insights they have to share, to themselves. Setting up a website and social media platforms and putting out their message this way can be a great way to find their audience, those who share their views and want to learn from them.

Summary

1. Great communicators and good at self-expression.
2. Words, whether written or spoken, are their gift and they know how to use them.
3. Can inspire people with the message they share, and light up a room.

4. Can be great teachers, writers and orators.
5. Online media is an easy vehicle for them to find their audience.
6. They need an audience – someone to listen to what they have to say!
7. Need to talk things out – not good at sorting it out in their heads.
8. Can channel in the moment.
9. It is important they are authentic in what they produce and share.
10. Need to beware talking for the sake of it, and offering unwanted advice.

Iris

Iris was the trusted messenger of the Greek Gods, and was the link between the world of men and the gods. She would travel by means of the rainbow, with which she became associated.

She had a shapeshifting energy, always choosing the best form from which to deliver her messages to mortals – maybe as a stranger, maybe as a friend. She is known as handmaiden to the Queen of Heaven, Hera and her husband Zeus.

Those with this energy centre could think of adopting Iris as their totem, and tuning into her energy as she delivers her messages from the gods, and how she chooses the best means to ensure the message is heard fully. Tuning in to this energy can ensure that the Fifth energy frequency soul uses its powerful gifts wisely and in service to the Divine.

6th Divine Soul Frequency
Divine Truth

Those born on this frequency, the energy of Divine Truth, have a gift for shining the light of Truth into dark corners. They use their insight and observational skills to get to the heart of what is happening and have the ability to convey the news succinctly.

So, Divine Truth is their gift, but it has to be stressed that this is the truth of their own individual Divinity – and is therefore highly subjective and personal to them.

Thus it is important that they are clear about what THEIR Truth is – and this is not their family, societies etc. but their own *individual* Truth. It is important to be VERY clear about this.

Those with this energy centre are spiritual warriors at heart and once they know their Truth they will make a strong stand for what they believe in – and bring Light in where it's needed.

Success will come when they are clear about and take a stand for their particular Truth, as well as helping others find and do the same for their Truth, helping them work out what is right for them individually. It cannot be stressed enough that those with this energy centre need to work out what THEY stand for, not the inputs of media, society, family etc, but what is really important to them – therefore they have to do their own research and not just swallow what main stream news outlets regurgitate.

It can also be a very useful exercise to refine exactly what their values are, and what they stand for.

Sixth frequency souls have the ability to bring the light of Truth to us all where needed, and as such can be incredibly valuable to the Collective if they are finding out what is *really* going on, rather than the official story.

They are the whistle blowers who will stand up for what they believe is right. They are really uncomfortable in an environment of lies and untruths and can spot a liar a mile off!

They are also highly visual and therefore have very good powers of observation, and have the ability to see both people and situations clearly – see the undercurrents and what lies beneath, what is really going on. They have the ability to get at the truth and sum it up in a few words.

As a consequence they clearly would make good investigative journalists, bloggers or documentary makers reporting on what lies behind the propaganda and lies that corporations, government and mainstream media use with great frequency to hoodwink the public, or maybe ferreting out the hidden truths about our origins and the many mysteries of life which mainstream teaching deliberately obfuscates. This is particularly useful at this moment in time when mainstream society is 'waking up' to the many lies, half-truths and inconsistencies we have been taught about and told through official sources of almost everything relating to our origins, history, abilities and reality etc.

Sixth frequency souls live in a highly visual world and are potentially highly intuitive and clairvoyant – gifts which if nurtured can become that of the visionary and seership. *This is like a muscle and needs to be used to be 'toned'* but is there as latent potential that can be worked with here.

Many Sixth frequency souls wish to work in very visual fields such as photography, art, visual arts and so on rather than use their gift for getting to the bottom of things in fields such as journalism, or even healthcare where the ability to target underlying health issues to bring about understanding of root healing can bring great benefit.

Consultancy work is also well suited as they can see what is needed and as a natural consultant and advisor they can carve a good career at this level in the business world. They will naturally be trusted if they are congruent and in integrity as people recognise their innate relationship with Truth, and their ability to help bring great clarity to an issue.

Sales – ethically-based of course - is also a good career path as their advice will be trusted, and coaching is another area where they will potentially shine. Within the corporate world both team members and bosses can benefit from their ability to speak the sometimes unpalatable Truth. They also have a great 'bullshit' radar, which can serve them well in many situations.

If they are congruent they will be a fearless champion for Truth – daring to name the elephant in the room and tell it like it is! They will dare to say what needs to be said and heard! It can take courage to do this, but it is a comprise of integrity to not speak their Truth when required.

There is a proviso here though – just blurting things out, regardless, can be disastrous. It is important they attract and surround themselves with people and groups who WANT this, value and want to hear what they have to say - even if it is unpalatable. Unfortunately not everybody either wants or is ready to hear the truth of a situation, particularly if it pops a much cherished bubble or is disadvantageous to them. So it is essential to choose their audience carefully – unless they are the proverbial whistle-blower, exposing cover-ups of course! Otherwise they will potentially be labelled 'conspiracy theorist', 'truther' or some other asinine label which will stand in the way of their message being heard by a greater audience.

They are most in alignment when they are sharing with those who appreciate them and the message they have to share. There are plenty who do not want to hear the Truth, or feel threatened by it and would rather live unconsciously or labouring under a delusion. It can be highly inconvenient to hear the Truth sometimes. So, if they want to use their gift to its fullest potential they have to ensure they have found the right audience, otherwise what they 'see' and 'know' will not be easily tolerated or valued.

This energy centre will need to develop diplomacy skills or check in with themselves and their environment before they blurt out unpalatable truths that will lose them friends and clients. It is important though that they are neither unnecessarily blunt nor overly diplomatic. Both ways the message can go unheard. They have to learn to speak a Truth in a way people can hear, without feeling threatened, criticised or judged – quite a balancing act!

Imbalance

This gift starts to go into imbalance often in childhood. They may well have been taught as a child 'we don't say that' or hushed up when they have come out with some devastatingly accurate but embarrassing observation in front of other. We can all remember times when a child has exposed the elephant in the room, to the great embarrassment of all concerned!

This causes confusion for the child, because they can see something clearly but they are being told to ignore it and not speak it, causing them to eventually keep what is so clear and obvious to them, to themselves rather than keep getting into trouble. They become silent, observing but not inter-acting, which is not making use of their gift to serve others in any way.

This confusion can lead the Sixth frequency soul to assume that people don't want to hear or can't handle what they have to say – but they must never assume this! Whilst it is true there may be those that don't want to hear, there are also plenty that do and will value highly their gift of reflecting a situation clearly back to others.

With maturity and awareness they can start to see how valuable it is to be truthful – even if diplomacy is required! – and become gifted in helping others navigate both tricky situations and soul growth.

It is important if and when they find themselves with someone to whom the Truth is unwelcome that they don't end up compromising their integrity in a situation or relationship where Truth isn't present. If they see/feel this happening they either need to re-negotiate or eliminate the relationship or situation before falling into incongruence.

They are out of integrity and alignment with their Divinity when lies, delusion and illusion are embraced in order to keep the peace or status quo. Not only is this damaging to them, but their astute powers of observation, keen radar for the reality of a situation and clarity of vision are compromised, a great loss of this gift to the world.

Dysfunctional

This energy centre becomes *very* dysfunctional when a shift is made from Truth into judgement. Everything becomes very black and white and rigid. They can start to think they know The Truth rather than their own subjective Truth and become dogmatic, entrenched and rigid in their thinking and quite aggressive and belligerent in the way this is communicated. This has the effect of alienating others even when they have something important to communicate, causes division and stagnation in any form of growth and will eventually leave them isolated as everyone steps back from those who are judgmental and righteous.

Taken further it can become more about being right rather than anything to do with Truth, and is totally out of alignment with their Divinity.

Summary

1. Help to bring the light of Truth to all.
2. Be succinct and communicate this with great clarity.
3. Truth is subjective –be clear what your *individual* Truth is, your core values and beliefs.
4. A fearless warrior for what You know to be right.
5. These are the whistle blowers and Truthers, uncomfortable around lies and deception.
6. Highly visual with good observation skills, you are human lie detector.
7. There is a latent ability for clairvoyance and seership, which can be developed.

8. Need to learn when it is appropriate to share and when not, learn diplomacy.
9. Shouldn't assume others aren't interested – find the right audience!
10. This gift becomes highly dysfunctional when it goes into judgment and rigid thinking.

Aletheia

Aletheia is the Greek goddess of Truth. She was a daughter of Zeus and personified the ideals of Truth and sincerity. She is a little known goddess, but she embodies some of the greatest challenges we as humans face to 'waking up' ie. seeing beyond the illusion.

Her name means 'truth' in the context of 'that which accords with reality' and she personifies truth as relating to and evidenced by facts which we can easily establish, should we care to look. Unfortunately, too few do, preferring the illusion fed to them by others, rather than establishing what *Is* for themselves.

Aletheia lent her name to the concept of re-membering and the state of being 'unhidden' ie. uncovering what is there to be found, what has been hidden or buried.

There are the great Truths of this Universe – the universal laws, the rhythms and cycles of nature and the cosmos and so on. Within this is the way we as humans can come to perceive these Truths and work with them.

It is interesting to note that within her name also lies the word '*lethe*' which means forgetfulness, oblivion, and is the river in the Underworld the souls returning to Earth had to drink from in order to forget their immortal nature. This is what we have to overcome to fully embody the true multidimensional glory of our Divinity within human form.

The Sixth frequency soul can find it useful, when they can clearly see a Truth many in the world don't want to acknowledge, to tune into Aletheia, and remember what she stands for. She is often pictured veiled (Truth hidden) or holding a mirror and the serpent of wisdom.

7th Divine Soul Frequency
Divine Power

The Seventh energy centre or frequency is that of Divine Power, which is accessed through free will and choice. It is important that this frequency needs to do and be whatever it wants to, without limitation as restriction, limitation, constraint or anything of this nature drains this energy centre quickly.

Having freedom of choice is incredibly important to the Seventh frequency soul – in fact freedom at every level is important to them! They are the archetypal free spirit who pushes against restraint and they hate being stuck in situations where they feel they have no choice, or their choices are very limited.

They need to avoid being boxed in at all costs and be given the freedom to choose, and to follow their choice.

This energy centre is energetically very sensitive and has an innate understanding of how energy works and how to use it and yet it is paradoxically likely that they may be unaware of this innate gift, thinking everyone has it, and underestimating its importance. This sensitivity means that they often retreat from people, finding it exhausting to be in crowds, noisy offices and so on.

They may also be very intuitive and psychic if this hasn't been shut down - and again, are unlikely to be fully aware of the depth of this gift, considering it to be 'normal'.

They are the energy conveyors, the energy receptors and the energy beacons in the room. Because they are so sensitive to the energy around them, it's important that they take time and space away from that noise and activity to recoup and regenerate, otherwise they will feel continuously frazzled.

If this energy centre is aligned they have the ability to manifest very quickly and powerfully. Results can happen fast and they can get what they want – and they tend to want it NOW! However, this ability to manifest very quickly only works when energy is flowing in alignment. If out of alignment what manifests is a whole lot of....nothing!

If what they are working on requires a lot of effort and feels like pushing water up hill, this frequency needs to learn to let go, as things aren't flowing. They need to really feel when things are in synch or they will not get the results they require. The earlier they learn this the more successful they can be in putting their considerable energy into the right things, rather than wasting time on those which will never work.

So it is important for them to know what they want and to be clear about this. It can't be someone else's version but genuinely theirs, their own vision, their own desire, their own goal, so they can tap into this soul frequency and make it become so in the world.

This is how they need to work – look at the feedback they get from the results they receive, what was wrong, out of tune, not aligned, disharmonious etc with what they were trying to do? Then they need to change what they do rather than keep doing the same old, same old that didn't work – things will not change just because they keep trying, but because they try a different tack.

So using their manifesting abilities is about honing a skill.

They can be impatient – they want what they want NOW! And if they are in alignment they will manifest quickly – but this also requires them to be sure of what it is they want, and not just work off whims or chasing bright glittery objects. The law of unexpected consequences can come in here.

The Seventh frequency soul understands better than most that making new choices creates new experiences, opens up new potentials, and they tend to find it easier than most to take action. This is especially true when they have learned to read the feedback from what they do – or don't –

manifest. This means that they also embrace change better than most when they can approach it from this angle.

They are also highly independent and strong-willed and can really make things happen when aligned, becoming the driving force that brings about change. When they learn to consciously create they can become a real force for good – or bad. Never forget it is just as easy to create destruction and negativity – it is always just a bad choice away.

A Seventh frequency soul can become a great force for good in the world, but has to have established a clear moral compass and integrity as well as their own clear vision of what they want to achieve. When all this is aligned they can become an unstoppable force.

They love tools and learning how to use them and see them as being a means of opening up new possibilities and new choices, expanding upon what is available to them. They love gathering up all sorts of things in their 'toolkit' as they work on the basis 'they never know when they'll need it' – a new software programme maybe, knowledge of new healing techniques, time-saving gadgets and so on, the possibilities are endless!

Childhood is often difficult for this energy centre as there is a strong push to self-determination and making their own choices – something most parents don't allow. This level of restriction and limitation is, at best, frustrating and at its worst can shut down a large part of their gift. Ideally a parent will allow them to explore and follow their curiosity whilst ensuring safe boundaries and self-discipline are established. A frustrated and restricted Seventh frequency child can become angry, even destructive, if too many strangleholds are put on them.

Money is also highly important – not for what it is but because of the freedom it brings with it.

They can also be a successful leader – they are strong willed, have lots of energy, are charismatic and attractive to others. They are willing to stick their neck out and go first, and others will follow....But again, this is what they need to choose, otherwise they will feel restricted and confined by a role that is not freely chosen.

In fact, their self-determination and their high energy levels makes them a natural leader, they can easily inspire others, but they need to learn to delegate – it can be too tempting to 'do it all' as they can get it done faster and more efficiently often than others. They can be frighteningly capable, but this becomes a burden and can lead to resentment and a sense of constraint if it all gets too much.

A balanced use of their power is to do what they want to do, accept the fact others don't work at their pace ….and delegate the rest!

They are not risk adverse, and are therefore more willing to fail than most, because they realise there are no bad decisions, just new experiences and that they can learn from their mistakes and do better next time.

People with this energy centre do best as entrepreneurs or working for themselves – they are in charge of what they do and how they do it, and can create what they want. Somebody else's rules and regulations just strangle them.

Seventh frequency souls are natural hands-on healers, but this gift often doesn't feel obvious to them. It usually takes a client's feedback to understand their power as healers as they often underestimate their power. Reiki is the perfect example of this. While everyone around them in training class is saying how they feel the energy as heat in their hands, or how they feel different once they are attuned, Seventh Energy Souls might quietly look on in envy as they don't feel any different! The truth is that they are likely to be more of a natural healer than most others, but don't 'feel' it, because, once again, it is so innate to them.

Imbalance

As has been stated, Seventh frequency souls are good leaders, but when out of alignment their leadership becomes manipulation and coercion and can be very damaging. They know how to use their charisma and psychology to use people in an unhealthy way. This is where we may first start to see this gift being corrupted, and where self-awareness needs to be cultivated.

This energy is pulled out of alignment by obligation – the musts, shoulds, have toos take away their freedom of choice, so anything that has this sense of obligation to it needs to be avoided. The worst possible situation to find themselves in is burdened with obligations, chores, responsibilities which they have not chosen and do not give them joy. And if a Seventh frequency soul finds themselves in such a situation they need to address it quickly or walk away. Otherwise they may find themselves doing ever more in order to establish some sort of sense of control so things can be done their way. Not that they want this....but if they have to it, at least they will have control will be their (faulty) thinking! In reality, they will find themselves drained, resentful and feeling trapped.

As they are high energy they can take on a lot, and often do – but they have to beware as it just might not be their responsibility or task to take on! They need to ask themselves is this really theirs to do? If they continue to tolerate obligation and let themselves get loaded up resentment starts to creeps in. They feel stifled and feel like they've had their wings clipped. This becomes very toxic in the long term, and comes back to the fact they need to establish what it is they want, their vision, their desires, their passion and work towards these goals. Nothing bests self-knowledge here.

They need freedom! Being accountable to others means they will become frustrated as they wait for others to do things or take action – it won't be at their pace and as time is another form of freedom the sense of things closing in will grow.

Just because they are capable and can doesn't mean they should. They need to heed this and only take on responsibility for things which they want to do. In fact, they should be their motto!

Dysfunctional

If a Seventh frequency soul does not respect their gift of energetic sensitivity it will come to feel like a burden to them and cause them to withdraw and become reclusive. If they get totally overloaded they will become dysfunctional to the extent that paralysis creeps in – they will be a busy fool, going round in circles, but never actually really doing or manifesting anything.

They will find that they are exploring new tools, new knowledge and so on, telling themselves they need this, but will not move forward or create something worthwhile with any of it – because there is something more they need to learn, or have, or do....

They will also find themselves getting stuck in indecision, whilst looking very busy whilst they are at it, working hard and long hours – but creating.....nothing! They are effectively spinning their wheels and not producing results.

A Seventh frequency soul needs to weed out all the obligations and responsibilities and areas where they feel they *should* do this or *must* do that, and come back to what they want to do – and focus on that!

Seventh frequency souls have excellent instincts and need to learn to trust their intuition and stick to their guidance as this will ensure their innate gifts are used both wisely and well.

Summary

1. The original free spirits.
2. Powerful manifestors and creators
3. Energetically very sensitive.
4. Can be very intuitive and psychic.
5. Action takers and can move and create fast.
6. Natural leaders and entrepreneurs.
7. Natural hands-on healers.

8. Need to steer clear of obligations, limitation and restrictions.
9. They need freedom.
10. Can become busy fools if they allow overwhelm to creep in.

Lilith

Lilith has been labelled as the original bad girl – the mother of demons no less! – by our patriarchal overlords, but the truth is her greatest sin was to want partnership, not ownership, from her husband Adam. She refused to 'lie under him' ie. accept his authority, or consent to a marriage that was not of her choosing, and for her sins she was banished from the Garden of Eden and vilified, with a compliant Eve being created to take her place.

Lilith married Samael, who is both said to be a fallen angel and somewhat confusingly to reside in 7th heaven! One assumes Samael was open to the concept of partnership Lilith required, and as such we then have an ancient powerful couple who represent an archetype well ahead of its time.

In the Sumerian/Babylonian tradition Lilith was the daughter of the Queen of the Netherworld, and consort to Enki-Samael. Together they made up what was called the Tree of Knowledge of Good and Evil, and they gave wisdom and knowledge to mankind.

Lilith is ancient, primordial and depending upon the ruling attitude was either seen as beneficial or evil. It is clear she is not a demonic force, she is the womb, the birthing force that is behind, amongst other things, the original primordial mother wisdom. She is a gatekeeper between worlds and connected to womb wisdom, a sacred warrior and protector who teaches there is nothing to fear in death.

Seductive, fierce, powerful she is death and rebirth, destruction and creation and above all, absolute love and compassion, here to uplift and serve us.

She is often depicted with horns – which denote receptivity to divine wisdom – and entwined with snakes, the serpents of wisdom. Seductive, fierce and powerful she is a force to be reckoned with.

Those with the frequency of Divine Power can resonate with this archetypal goddess, who despite millennia of smears, can show us what it is to stand in one's power, complete and unashamedly herself.

8th *Divine Soul Frequency*
Divine Wisdom

The Eighth soul frequency is that of Divine Wisdom.

Divine Wisdom is about an inherent connection to the universal wisdom of the Cosmos as it relates to the physical world.

Wisdom and knowledge are not the same things....nor are Wisdom and Truth. Truth is subjective, Wisdom is universal and comes from a deep inner gnosis, not outer learned knowledge.

With a predominant Eighth frequency these souls have a direct connection and inherent understanding of this universal wisdom, and as a result tend to be thoughtful, introspective and an excellent listener.

They are the person people come to when they want good advice or insight into a problem as they have a gift for being able to give amazingly insightful, succinct advice which is rooted in common sense and rational thinking, and somehow gets to the heart of the issue.

Those are both gifts they have – common sense and rational thinking. There is nothing common about common sense! It is a gift that others are aware of and value.

They also tend to grasp concepts and ideas based on spiritual wisdom and truths quickly and easily and can help others come to an understanding of it. In fact, as they open to this gift their connection to the universal wisdom and energy grows and deepens and their awareness of other levels of being expands.

Of immense value to the Collective is the fact that they have the facility to express these great concepts succinctly and in a way that enables others to grasp and understand it. This is a great gift that has the power to help others open to their Divinity and Divine purpose.

Eighth frequency souls can 'see' or 'feel' when people are trying to run a bypass on reason and logic in what they are thinking, or the story they are telling themselves., and when it badly begins to diverge from what is wise.

This enables them to understand how they can help others to understand where their thinking is not making sense or has tipped over into wishful thinking. Obviously this needs to be handled diplomatically but in the right hands can save much wasted time and effort.

They can also help others course-correct in order to align with Divine Wisdom and the principles of Universal Law, which are often not obvious to the majority.

The principles of Natural Law and Universal Law are 'felt' by an aligned Divine Wisdom soul as a strong and guiding force within their life. These principles do not have to be taught to them, they innately understand them.

Wisdom is very concise – they do not necessarily have a lot to say, but what they do say is usually profound. This is why others listen to them. It is rare to find an Eighth frequency soul who indulges in idle chit chat, but the little they say carries depth and meaning. So although this energy frequency is usually not a big talker, when they do speak, they are worth listening to. They don't value trite conversations or being drawn into 'small' talk. When it comes to decision-making they are deliberate and thoughtful, they do not make poorly thought out decisions or judgments, but are considered in the opinions and decisions they do come to, often tapping into their Divine connection to check they are aligned.

They have a gift for helping others see through their own illusions, false self-perceptions and faulty thinking – as a consequence they would make an excellent coach or trainer in the self-development/spiritual world as well as being good at managing teams, or even having a career in ethical sales. They listen patiently, work ethically and can impart the insight and wisdom they have to offer succinctly.

Intelligent, highly principled and with thinking based in reason, with their level of insight, they also make very good negotiators and diplomats. They will tend to embrace logic and common sense over emotionality and have the ability to reduce complex things down to a level of simplicity that is easy for most to comprehend and get to the nub of something.

They are also very good at working out the simplest, quickest and most efficient way to get from A to B to achieve a goal or an aim. They can be a valuable team member on any kind of project.

Imbalance

The negative polarity of this energy centre is irrationality – they do not thrive in environments or situations where reason and common sense either does not prevail or is not valued or present. Things need to make sense to them – if something is illogical or doesn't make sense they will struggle to comprehend why people want to do it.

This can frustrate them more than most as they really don't 'get' it, and they will either become frustrated and angry or withdraw from engaging when natural wisdom and common sense seem to have flown out of the window in favour of reckless foolishness.

Sometimes there may be a desire to detach from Society and all that doesn't make sense. Often Society and its laws and dictates do not follow Divine Wisdom and Natural Law which leaves them frustrated and even angry. Stepping back from this is a defense mechanism and although understandable, it can be a shame as they have a lot of wisdom to impart and guidance to give to others if they can stick with the mainstream.

A child of this frequency who incarnates to parents who don't operate reasonably, finds it very difficult and confusing.

The strategy for Eighth frequency souls is not to put themselves into situations that don't make sense – they must either address or eliminate situations and relationships that come under this heading. Reason, logic and common sense that align to Divine Wisdom must be present and valued or they will become very impatient and fed up. The more they are exposed to this the more these feelings will spill over and they will start to relate to people in general through this lens becoming irritable, short-tempered and snappy.

Dysfunctional

When this frequency becomes very dysfunctional it results in feeling contempt for Society and others in the way they work, and once this happens wisdom may shift into a form of spiritual and intellectual arrogance.

They may also withdraw from the world, staying on the outside of social conventions, groups and so on as they become angry and intolerant of a world where no-one seems to listen or operate from logic and common sense!

Here their gift becomes wasted, as they don't share their wisdom and insight to help make the world a better place.

The Eighth frequency soul needs to create relationships and situations where their natural wisdom and insight are valued, and move on from those which don't honour this.

Summary

1. Direct connection to universal wisdom.
2. Have an inherent understanding of universal concepts of wisdom.
3. Thoughtful, concise, principled, and excellent listeners.
4. Gifted with common sense and rational thinking.

5. Can clearly see where others are out of alignment with their divinity and help them course correct.
6. Embrace logic and common sense over emotionality.
7. Not into small talk or trite conversations – their conversation carries depth.
8. If things don't make sense they can find life difficult and will ultimately detach if they remain in this environment.
9. Need to work and live in environments where their common sense and rationality and inner wisdom are valued.
10. They live in alignment to Universal Laws and can help others do the same, becoming great role models for others.

Sophia

Sophia is the feminine personification of wisdom. She embodies gnosis, that form of inner knowing which is not about learnt knowledge, but direct connection to universal wisdom and laws. As Wisdom Incarnate, she is also the Wisdom of Deity.

In Biblical terms she is seen as being the feminine face of God, but every culture has her equivalent within it – in Greece, Athena, in Sumeria, Inanna, in Buddhism, Tara and so on.

As the feminine element of the Divine she is the nurturing element of the life force. She is the Source of Wisdom, and from her came the material world. She is the keeper of all that is righteous and just, and those who follow her guidance prosper.

Unfortunately, the majority of Mankind ignore her and her gifts. It is said she was born of Silence, and only those who truly seek her find her and

the abundant gifts she has to offer. Where she is absent in someone's life darkness and ignorance flourish. She brings understanding, insight and spiritual exploration to those who seek her, and introduces the spiritual into the material world.

Those with the frequency of Divine Wisdom can tune into her energy to hone and enhance their own Divinity and strengthen their connection to this flow of energy.

Part Two -
Starseed Families

Starseed Families Introduction

All souls in this Universe emanate initially from the great fields of sound and light which are Harmonic Universe or Density 5 and are 'birthed' into different dimensions and different races across the universe.

For a newly minted soul this is considered the point of origin, and a new soul may spend all its time in its birth system, with its birth race (it may well be in an immortal form, depending upon what frequency it is vibing at and its DNA potential and activation) or it may chose at some point to go off and experience other systems and other races, either by direct galactic travel, or by choosing to move their soul into another incarnation cycle in another system, maybe in a different Density. They may even choose to take on a 'mission' as part of the Guardian Alliance[4] undertakings to help any race and any being back into alignment with God Source and restore its genetic potentiality, even if it has been deliberately altered.

We have here on planet Earth Starseeds from many Starseed families from across our Universal Time Matrix. Many have come to experience reincarnation and activate their spiritual mission for a wide variety of reasons, but for most the primary reason at this particular point in our planetary cycle is to establish freedom on this planet from the forced reincarnation mechanics which have been installed here by digressed galactic races to keep Souls from evolving, and to restore the Angelic Human DNA blueprint which has been deliberately badly messed with, and allow once more the natural evolution of consciousness on this planet.

---

[4] See Appendix C

In short, most starseeds are here 'on mission' to help Angelic humanity free themselves from the clutches of those fallen races who took over planet Earth and have attempted to enslave us.

There are many reasons as to why and how this has happened which are part of both galactic history and the history of our human origins, but this is a story too vast to sum up in a few sentences and too complex to go into here, but a fascinating topic for another book.

Both benevolent and malevolent extraterrestrial races have been involved with this planet for many millions of years, and still are. Humanity, as a whole, was aware of this until around 5,500 years ago, when a Collective mind wipe was implemented on the planetary consciousness grids, and we were all fed a different story of our history and origins – remember the winner writes history and the 'histories' we have been given within the education we now receive do not reflect in any way the reality of human history.

Many Starseeds came here on 'reconnaissance' missions and found themselves caught in the consciousness traps put in place. Many others have come in to both rescue these and humanity so they can either return to their home frequencies or, in the case of Earth, ascend to the next density as was part of the plan for humanity's evolution.

All Starseeds are endeavoring to anchor in and hold here on the planet higher and higher levels of frequency to permit this to happen as well as grounding into the planetary grids energetic codes and frequencies. As these energies are being exposed to the planetary grids and all those connected to these grids are affected – humans, animals, plants etc.

Starseed Souls have lived and originate from other planetary systems as has been said. It some cases it is other galaxies and other dimensions within this Time Matrix, and in a few cases from interlocking God Worlds or Time Matrices beyond this one.

They are all here to assist in bringing to a successful completion the Stellar Ascension Cycle we are currently in, enabling Earth to move to the next stage of her evolution.

Starseeds come into a human body at birth normally. A few are walk-ins.[5] Some are born knowing their identity and purpose, others are to be activated, or wake up, at a later time. The timing of the moment of birth is deliberate and orchestrated with specific coding within the DNA blueprint. Souls agreeing to come to Earth also need to find corresponding genetics that fit their soul's mission, and are also programmed with a spiritual mission and higher purpose to aid in the activation of their brothers and sisters here on the planet.

Once a Starseed comes into knowledge and alignment of their mission and purpose here on Earth they come into their full potential, so the 'waking up' and activation of Starseeds is important in this respect. It has been noted that there seems to be a constant among Starseeds, which is that a higher guidance system oversees their stay on Earth and assists when truly needed and is connected to a larger group spiritual purpose.

Starseeds, as a group, have been heavily targeted by the Fallen Races, often referred to as the Dark Forces or negative aliens, that are here on

---

[5] Walk-in – a Soul who comes into a mature human body with the permission of the consciousness already inhabiting this body. This can be because there is an urgent need to convey some information or fulfil a purpose and there is not the time to go through the normal routes and wait for maturity so another consciousness 'lends' them the mature vehicle in order to do what is required.

this planet and have their own agenda, with superimposed karmic loads, implants, deliberate tampering or interference and the use of drugs and various chemicals to ensure at the very least there are immense difficulties with coming into a place of alignment with their mission, or at worst a total derailment!

Often the path of a Starseed on this planet is not easy!

But – as many Starseeds note – it is precisely these challenges that often help us to 'wake up' and quickly learn the need to keep our energies clean and clear so we can recover from the derailment of our mission.

The following information on different Starseed groups is by no means definitive, but expresses the best that I am aware of at this moment. As the veils thin and we are recovering the knowledge and memories that were taken from us, we are remembering more and more. This process has only just begun, but I hope what you find here will stimulate your own remembering and knowing, and expansion of this knowledge.

Some groups have been interacting with the Earth through many ages, and we know more about these, who are often fairly close neighbours. Others are here only in small numbers, and from distant systems we know little about. But more is coming through all the time.

Who knows? You may be able to add to what is here at some point yourself.

How Do You Know If You Are A Starseed?

I know of no quick and easy quiz to take to establish your Soul's point of origin.

The information is held within the planets morphogenetic fields at the 5th dimensional level and beyond within what is called the planetary Akash. In order to access the Akashic records it is necessary to be able to access the 5th dimension at a minimum and trace the necessary information.

There are various ways to do this and a wide variety of excellent teachers now instructing others in the process.

Or you could commission a report or reading from one of the many trained readers who offer their services.

A Brief Word on the Negative or Fallen Races

The Fallen Races are spread throughout the galaxy and have infiltrated almost every sector, star system and race – contrary to popular beliefs there are negative Pleiadians, Sirians, Lyrans, Arcturians etc. So always beware if a being contacts you claiming to want to help at this time – is it from the Guardian Races, is it God, Sovereign, Free and does it have a 12-strand or beyond DNA templating?

Fallen Races have a maximum of 11-strand DNA with some having less. So beware being tricked.

Their interactions with humanity are usually based on deception, trickery, misinformation, misrepresentation and more nefarious activities besides. Many communicate through well-intentioned human channels in order to mislead and deceive, and many well-intentioned people are being coached in harmful and soul destructive techniques under the guise of Ascension or spiritual ideologies.

For an awakening Starseed it can be easy to be sent off course by teachers and sources who are unknowingly being led astray themselves. The New Age movement has been badly infiltrated at this level.

I do not want to go into great detail about the Fallen Race lineages and their negative agendas here as it is not the appropriate place, but knowledge of them definitely helps in sorting out the wheat from the chaff. Suffice it to say that not every contact from a Pleiadian being or a Sirian being etc, etc, is benign with a core intent to help humanity progress, evolve and heal – some are, the majority are not!

Here I am focusing on Starseeds, and these are galactic beings who have chosen to incarnate on Earth into a human body at this time as part of a great movement to get Earth and her many life forms out of the mess in which they find themselves, through no fault of their own. So I will not focus on the Fallen races but want you to be aware that you need your bullshit radar turned up high all the time, and be aware that you are constantly in danger of being tricked.

Star Family - The Blueprinter Family

Blueprinters are unusual in that they, as a group, are not defined by a specific location but are 'Star Travellers' and energetic 'engineers' of sorts. They are a group of souls who have been instrumental in both designing and engineering the human experience of the Divine Blueprint on Earth as a place for Divine self-expression.

It is impossible for a Blueprinter to realise their originating point without awareness of the 15D Time Matrix within which we live as they emanate originally from these consciousness fields which have to be vastly stepped down to come into form.

Blueprinters are very advanced Souls that emanate from HU4 and HU5, and the frequency of consciousness has, of necessity, been stepped down many times in order to enter this density and dimensional level. They are emanations of the architects and creators of life within this God World, come into embodiment for a variety of purposes.

They carry the Blueprint and codes for embodying Spirit consciously and for experiencing Creation through the physical body.

Occasionally you may come across a Blueprinter who has a strong connection to a particular system in their energy field, often because they have spent a lot of time there.

I, myself, am a Blueprinter, and have found this gives me a rather unique perspective on both galactic history and some of the stories that various races tell about themselves within it. Once you can reconnect to the sourcing consciousness from which you came it enables the lifting of the amnesia and miasms that are part of incarnating here on the planet to be cleared much quicker, but it is not an overnight process. The physical body has to 'learn' to hold ever higher levels of frequency without harming it.

Blueprinters are heavily targeted if they are identified as incarnating in order to shut them down and keep them that way. But this is a challenge faced by almost all Starseeds and just one of the many difficulties we all encounter.

So, Blueprinters do not identify with any particular place in the cosmos but work throughout the cosmos getting consciousness into physical form. They work in direct connection with, and have a mandate from Source to design the consciousness blueprint(s) throughout the Universe. They specialise in originating various dimensions of Creation wherever you may find them. Earth is just one of these 'projects', but it is an advanced one, so let's take a moment to look at what Earth School is about.

The Original Blueprint for Life on this planet, was seeded here aeons ago by the Blueprinters, coming direct from Source. Blueprinter souls carry ancient wisdom within them and understand how the Universal energies work - the more esoteric and metaphysical aspects of learning we have here on Earth will make complete sense to them, they carry the memory of this within. They are magical, creative and deeply wise.

Some of the many instructions sets in the Earth Blueprint is to experience

Spirit through physicality, and to live through the mastery and coming together of the physical, emotional, mental and spiritual realms which the human blueprint can access, living inter-dimensionally, consciously and fully connected to Spirit whilst in physical form. The Angelic Earth human was also given the genetic coding to be the guardians of the consciousness grids and Stargates of this solar system – a mission which has gone badly astray.

The Earth Blueprint is formed round a 12-strand Diamond Sun DNA template, which is designed to allow the angelic human who activates this template to move fully in physical form through the dimensional levels of the Time Matrix via the Star gates. It also holds the potential from there to expand into what is called the Double Diamond Sun template (24 strand) and even eventually into a 48 strand template, which is the level of the great creator Collectives of consciousness of this Matrix.

You may have heard that humanity has the potential to be creator gods – this is what is meant.

It is not a little thing. Blueprinters are very experienced in the realm of Creation and yet this particular type of Blueprint has not been assayed before. As I said, it is a very advanced Blueprint. Mistakes have been made in the learning of how to deliver this, and digressed and Fallen races which have a particular agenda and hatred of the potential of the DNA template are doing all they can to scupper the success of the experiment, but there are many Blueprinters here on Earth at this time, along with many, many other Starseeds from benevolent races, to help shift the Blueprint back to its original purity.

Some of these mistakes have come about by Blueprinters not fully understanding what it is to be in a physical human body, which is very different to working in realms of higher frequencies. There has also been an unforeseen anomaly in the way the emotional body has interacted with the more animalistic, survival driven instincts of the physical body, especially due to the fact probably the vast majority of the planet holds some alien coding in their DNA due to the experiments deliberately carried out by the negative aliens which have caused so much chaos here.

This has meant that human emotional responses and interactions are a much larger part of the human experience than foreseen and mastery of the emotional body harder as a result to achieve for the majority. This emotional response is rather a wild card, and Blueprinters struggle to understand and predict what will happen. Many Blueprinters at the 'down and dirty' end of making the Blueprint happen incarnate into a human body and have a steep learning curve to get a handle on the emotional aspects of being human. And in addition there is the deliberate manipulation and interference in the genetics and DNA templating to unravel also.

Thought is translated into action or made manifest through the frequency of emotion. A thought creates a feeling, and it is this feeling which moves us to action....or not. For example, we might think 'I would like a cup of tea', but it is the emotional response to that – either 'mmmm, yes' or 'can't be bothered' which has us getting up and making the effort to make that cup of tea.

Ensuring that emotion is running at the right frequencies for the higher outcomes is challenging. And much of the current need is to raise the Collective frequency field to one where the higher frequencies of emotion predominate, not the lower ones of fear, anger, shame and so on.

This is not as straightforward as it sounds, as there are unfortunately Beings in the Universe who like things just the way they are on Planet Earth, and are trying to prevent the realignment with the original Blueprint and genetic coding.

None of this is helped by the fact that Free Will is also part of the Earth Blueprint – another wild card!

This has resulted in Blueprinters incarnating into physicality here on Earth in order to both understand and guide the Blueprint back to its original form. Blueprinters often struggle with understanding the human experience in its totality as this is not their natural form, and it takes time to understand how to behave, understand emotional responses etc in order to fit in.

To enable a return to the Original Blueprint there has to be a remembrance held of it and part of what Blueprinters are on Planet Earth to do is to hold this remembrance open for others to access –quite a difficult task as like every soul coming into physical incarnation Blueprinters have to first wake up themselves to who they are and what they are here to do.

There are times in Earth's great cycles where the energetic environment which our solar system finds itself in is such that big evolutionary leaps and upgrades of consciousness are possible. We have just entered into one of these phases at this moment and many Blueprinters have incarnated at this time to ensure the necessary realignments can be made.

As co-creators of humanity Blueprinters have a karmic tie and deep connection to Earth and will keep returning here in order to help evolve consciousness according to the Original Blueprint. They are helping to guide not just humanity's evolution, but also that of the planet and its other Life forms.

It is essential that Blueprinters remember and reconnect to who they are as it is needed to maintain connection to other Beings who are off-planet/in other dimensions who are assisting in the delivery of the Earth Blueprint and helping guide its unfolding. This is the equivalent of a 'Blueprint Committee' of Beings all wanting to ensure the best possible outcome for delivery of the Earth Blueprint.

Blueprinters are said to be make up about 8% of the world population at this moment – a sign of the evolutionary and exciting times we are in! There are six different types of sub-groups of Blueprinter souls. Each specialises in a particular aspect of designing and delivering the Blueprint, and not all will seek to incarnate in a physical body in order to do so. So let's look at each in turn.

Blueprint Originators

These specialise in the development of the original design. They are the original architects of the Plan if you like. Other Blueprinters will take on the task of implementing it. Blueprint Originators are only ever likely to come to Earth at times of major potential or shift, such as the one we find ourselves in at the moment.

They will ensure they are birthed into affluent families in positions of influence, to get the best of education and opportunities. They will be in positions of power and prominence. They are not here for the human experience or to worry about day-to-day survival, but to influence humanity at the level of the global scale of uplifting humanity.

They come to bring in and hold the light codes of the Original Blueprint and to understand some of the original distortions which have occurred in order to heal them. They have worked with this Blueprint for eons. They have endless devotion and dedication to Earth.

There are very few Originators here in incarnation at any time – even those such as now. They are here to guide and to influence the adjustment of the Codes at the macro scale.

They tend to be observers, or work behind the scenes influencing changes, or trying to shift perspectives and usually hold themselves apart, being free of the same need to belong as say an Earther does.

Like all Blueprinters, being in physicality is difficult and if there is a dysfunctional aspect to this particular group it is that they can become disenchanted with the struggle they face to bring humanity back into alignment with the plan. Humanity is taking a long time to embrace consciousness (mainly due, in fairness, to the deliberate interference it has endured from fallen races) and shows itself all too willing to get lost within illusions rather than clearly see reality and embrace this.

Blueprint Designers

Blueprint Designers are the aestheticians. They bring beauty to the Blueprint – and with Planet Earth and its lifeforms we can see that they have excelled themselves. They work closely with, and have many traits in common with the Blueprint Originators.

These are highly creative souls who take what is functional and make it beautiful and have an innate understanding of energy flows and geometries of sound and light.

Much like the Originators, very few come into physical incarnation, and those that do tend to hold themselves apart. They are the reclusive artists, who live for what they do, their art energetically having the ability to contribute to raising the level of consciousness on the planet.

Like many, they can struggle however, with the practical, strictly 3D aspects of life as a human – relationships, paying bills, social niceties and conventions and such like. If they are dysfunctional it is due to the fact they may get lost in what they do, they live for their art, and all else passes them by.

Blueprint Technicians

Blueprint Technicians are what we would liken to the engineers of the process of delivering the Blueprint – after all, someone had to figure out how to step energy down into physical form in a way which works. So structures such as the energy body, chakra system, meridians, and the whole interface with the physical body through the nervous and endocrine system is part of what they would address. The DNA, a masterful means of programming physical structure as well as accessing the information field, is also part of their work.

So the way a human being and other life forms work is part of their remit. They are happy to delve into the detail and figure out how to optimise the way it all functions. As you can imagine, it is no little thing to work out how to bring consciousness into form.

Technicians who incarnate are very logical, rational and mentally orientated. They are not necessarily highly emotionally intelligent (although they might dispute this!) and tend to rationalise their emotions. They want to know how things function and will be drawn to any areas where the focus is on how things function, whether it be mindset, classic engineering or medical research for instance. They are very detail-oriented, and have to beware getting bogged down at this level. They need to pull back and see the big picture on occasion.

Highly intelligent, there can be a tendency towards arrogance and a know-it-all attitude which does not endear them to others. Here in deep physicality they can forget that there is a spiritual element which runs through everything and become the scientists of the 'only if I can see it, feel it, touch it' variety. Because they are very mind-based and detail oriented, they can miss the big picture, able to see – and point out – where others are failing, but unable to apply the same insight to themselves.

Of course, not all Technicians are like this. The more evolved the soul the more likely it will be able to integrate body, mind and spirit as well as develop understanding and facility with the feeling self.

Blueprint Translators

Blueprint Translators undertake the task of translating the codes of the Blueprint into forms which work at the human level, whether that be mental, emotional, physical or spiritual. So they will look at the raw materials they have to work with and see how they can be formulated into a usable form or function for Planet Earth. Once this has been figured out it is up to the next Blueprinter group – the Deliverers, to ensure it happens.

So their major function is to formulate the codes for Earth's Blueprint that can be moved into form. As I have mentioned, the Earth Blueprint is unique, and has to be translated into frequencies that work here in deep physicality. But they also work with the frequencies of other Star Families who have come to Earth to help with what is unfolding, so they are figuring out how the unique gifts of these groups can best be used for the benefit of all.

The Translators are the problem solvers, as they need to deliver solutions that not only work well at the level of physicality, but also ensure that the Blueprint translation is as pure as possible – and they need to ensure that it is as safe from misuse and abuse as it can be, as there are Beings in the galaxy who have other agendas going on.

Bringing Light and Life into form is not straightforward!!

So the Blueprint Translators who incarnate on Earth tend to be very practical and will often be found in areas such as computer programming and development, spiritual development, and even innovative health and wellness counsellors or even food chefs. Any area that helps to bring humanity back into alignment with the original Blueprint and DNA template will attract them. They will always be figuring out how things can be improved, and taking concepts and ideas and finding ways to make them manifest in form.

Translators are very committed and responsible and still have a lingering sense of guilt over the fact that the Blueprint went awry some millennia ago. It lost its purity and they can still feel responsible for this, and feel helpless and frustrated in the face of trying to ensure a return to the perfection of the original Blueprint, in the face of what often seems to be overwhelming odds, even though most of the problems were caused by the unauthorised interference of others.

Blueprint Deliverers

The Blueprint Deliverers were the first Blueprinter souls to incarnate into human physicality and they are very much involved in trying to promote consciousness from within the human experience as well as ensure humanity keeps and develops a strong connection to the Divine.

They are literally here to deliver the Blueprint!

Many Blueprint Deliverers have had many, many incarnations here on the Earth (right from the first seeding) and there is a possibility that they have become rather caught up in the mixed up, confused process of physicality to the extent that the energies of Divine Love, compassion, kindness, respect etc which they embody and can radiate are often hidden beneath past traumas.

But their memory of the Blueprint and the Divine Love which permeates it is held within their soul memory, and if they overwhelmed by the experience of physicality they need to find a way to get back in touch with this aspect of themselves to restore their ability to deliver the Blueprint

They tend to be drawn to the less conscious aspects of human society, where their particular gifts are most needed, and work in ways within this to help promote greater levels of consciousness – think social workers, educators, charitable organisations, healthcare givers for example.

They literally get into the body to help deliver the blueprint and can be very hands on in the way they work!

They are very inclusive – they want everybody to have access to the same resources and equality of opportunity, this is very important to them.

Throughout history they have promoted human rights and equality, often to the detriment of their well-being.

Blueprint Deliverers hold a strong belief that abundance is the natural birthright of every being, human or otherwise, on this planet. They nurture and feed in whatever way they can anything that will help ensure that all can access the abundance which is inherent in the Blueprint codes for this planet.

They know the transformational quality of Divine Love and that anything is possible if this is present.

They have to beware trying to help people who really don't want to be helped – and there are plenty of these around, stuck deep in their own stories and victimhood, or caught deep within the clutches of fallen race machinations. Engaging with this will only drain them. They have to learn to move on and find those who are genuinely open and ready for their help.

They have to realise that many people do not want or are not ready to accept the responsibility of empowerment and are literally choosing unconsciousness. Trying to help these people to wake up will just exhaust them and leave them frustrated.

They can get overwhelmed by considering the levels of unconsciousness, inequality etc on this planet, leaving them feeling very disempowered. The danger of this is that they can sink into the level of consciousness they are here to change – an 'if you can't beat them join them' attitude. Their innate sensitivity can be a problem at this level.

Being in a disempowered environment for too long can be unhelpful. They can choose difficult environments – charity workers, mental health, aid workers, etc and they need to have a strategy to dip in and out regularly so they can recharge.

Blueprint Changers

Blueprint Changers can be likened to the trouble shooters who go in and help to clean up some of the more difficult and potentially darker aspects of human experience that have been thrown up by the distortions to the Blueprint.

Souls on Earth at the moment are in deepest polarity and illusion – there is the potential for great joy and illumination but also for deep anger and other negative emotions.

Humans needs to re-establish quickly at this time higher levels of consciousness, having been deliberately 'put to sleep' and the Blueprint Changers are tasked with helping with this. They are the healers of body, mind and emotions and have great empathy for suffering.

As a consequence they often take incarnations that are very difficult – ie sexual abuse, victimization, war, violence etc so they can bring consciousness to these areas on the planet. They are the classic role models who experience great trauma, overcome it and are then able to show others the path through the suffering.

It goes without saying that they have a survivor's compassion if they can open themselves to the suffering of others.

Another aspect of the Blueprint Changer's gift is they bring with them the message that life is a gift and to be enjoyed, despite all its challenges and traumas. They remind us that Life is precious and to be savoured, not just endured, and can bring a real shot of life energy into those who are soul weary.

Their greatest challenge is to not get lost in the human experience and become the victim themselves of their situation, becoming drained and burdened by the role they have taken on. It is essential they remember their greater purpose and overcome the situation and inspire others

---

through their example – they become the role model of how to rise above it.

Embracing a 'cause' they have overcome themselves is very powerful for them. Indeed, they are very powerful souls, helping others overcome their difficulties and find the way to their purpose. This path leads to abundance for them and others.

'Being the Change' is important to this group in particular, to ensure they don't get caught up in the 'story', thus failing to bring new consciousness to dysfunctional areas of life.

Star Family - Alpha Caeli

Alpha Caeli is a double star in the Caelum constellation. Caeli is pronounced 'si-lai' and Caelum 'si-lem'. Its name in Latin means the Chisel and describes a sculptor's chisel.

This group of Earth Starseeds has only recently been recognised so we do not have a lot of information about them. There are still very few of them here although they have been helping humanity from the 'other side' for many years.

They have mainly been working at the non-physical level with traumatised souls once they pass over – they are superb healers and help souls 'detox' traumatic life experiences. It is only in the last millennia that they have started to incarnate into physicality as well. This was partly by extremely dedicated souls who felt they needed to understand 'from the inside' what exactly life on Earth was like so they could be more effective in their healing, and partly because they felt they could be of more service in the upcoming times by being here on Earth physically.

As interdimensional light beings they were of a 7th dimensional frequency and Earth is very low density compared to this. Despite this there is a quality of lightness they carry with them, relating to their soul's high frequency.

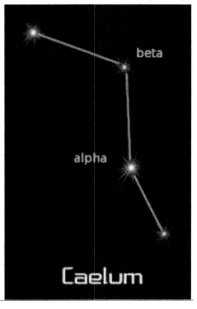

Not surprisingly they can struggle somewhat here on Earth to find their feet. This can lead to an Alpha Caelian Starseed feeling somewhat like a fish out of water. The deep polarities which are so intrinsic to Earth – positive and negative, dark and light – can be a real struggle for them to deal with. This can lead to a lack of confidence, of self-assurance, as they feel they should be able to cope with this easily, after all they can help others so why not themselves?

And they do help others. They are very effective healers, very sensitive empaths (which can be difficult!) and they are beautiful souls who uplift those they have dealings with. It is just they under-estimated somewhat the difficulty and density of life of Earth.

It takes great courage to come from a high frequency and deliberately take on a lower one with all its intrinsic difficulties. Alpha Caelians need to remember this when they are beating themselves up for struggling to cope. They are showing us through their example how to build a gentler, kinder, more inclusive society and that is no little thing.

Star Family - Alpha Centauri

Alpha Centaurians are our near neighbours, they are the closest star to us - just 2.5 light years away!

And they are good neighbours, Earth's self-appointed guardians, who started coming in around 50,000 years ago and are still here contributing what they can. The threat has changed, but their mission hasn't.

They are inherently compassionate souls and are fully invested in helping humans out of the current dilemma they are in. Their Collective mission is to protect Earth against negativity and negative interference.

Earth was originally – and is now to some extent – mainly populated by young souls, and there was a naiveté around buying into the disruptive energies and the consequences of that. The deliberately disruptive use of light and sound codes which characterise the negative alien influence on the planet creates a negative, lower frequency power field, and Alpha Centaurians are here to raise the frequency sufficiently to stop this negative use, thus helping people connect with the Divine light within.

In addition, there are beings here on Earth which seek to drain the life force from others, using it as energy for themselves. This is against cosmic law and these light or energy vampires do not have permission to get their Life force from others. The Alpha Centaurians have encountered these beings before and help Earth souls come into their own power to prevent this.

Alpha Centaurians bring a kind of self-sufficiency to the equation. They have an unwavering connection to

Source, and this absolute connection to Universal Love energy not only makes people feel safe and protected around them but helps them remember that the Creator holds us all and that Love and abundance is available if we just find our way to connecting with it.

Alpha Centaurians are fearless as they recognise that true power lies within – it is a choice to give that power to an external source like a leader or a terrorist (or a virus!). They are not afraid of the so-called external threat or the illusion of power it may hold, and they can thus help others to see through this illusion and retain their power.

They are here to help us dismantle the various abusive systems of power which have been constructed, whether it be medical systems, banking systems, corporate or political systems, legal systems, energy companies, drug companies or the myriad other systems that seek to keep people poor, fearful and disempowered. Wherever there is corruption they will be seeking to expose this – and there is much for them to engage with at this moment in time.

Alpha Centaurian Souls have a high mental ability and the capacity to hold a high level of consciousness. They are visionaries, they see the big picture – but are not much good with the detail. They bring forth new ideas, inspiration, new possibilities. They are seed planters, but hand over to others the watering and harvesting. They are not good at follow through, always looking to the next horizon, the next thing to learn, explore, figure out. They want to move on, bring in a new vision, whilst holding to Source connection. They are like a tuning fork to a higher vibration, leading humanity forwards to better, more inclusive, more aligned ways of being in the world.

As I have said, Alpha Centaurians have high mental abilities and are much more comfortable operating from their mental body than their emotional. They have an affinity to technology, are analytical, great problem solvers, and often possess a very disciplined work ethic. This combined with their visionary skills means they can give a huge helping hand in advancing our science and technological know-how, and bringing it into a more harmonious expression with the planet and nature.

Their strong practical streak has an emphasis on functionality. Their focus is on function rather than form. Very protective, Alpha Centaurians are strong and dependable and can be relied on, and are very strong, steadfast people that roll up their sleeves and do what needs to be done. Needless to say, they are excellent providers for their families.

The area where Alpha Centaurians may struggle is with their emotional body. The emotional perspective is often lost on them, they may struggle to name and process what they are feeling. Whilst they understand emotions conceptually and intellectually they are not necessarily very good at feeling them.

They also are not known for being physically very demonstrative, instinctively wanting to keep their energy fields as pure as possible.

There are times where this lack of emotional involvement can be a strength – by not being emotionally engaged in a drama some Alpha Centaurians can become experts at helping others sort out their feelings and emotional bodies. So some career areas are counselling, coaching and healing professions where they just hold a clear space for others to sort out their emotions. This obviously requires a good understanding of emotions even if they are not empathic and don't 'feel' them strongly themselves.

This may make them seen uncaring – they are not. Far from it! But they are self-contained.

The danger is though that some Alpha Centaurians have a tendency to ignore the emotional body completely, both for themselves and in others – they don't feel it and they act as if others don't either. Some literally have to 'learn' the type of behaviour patterns and acts which demonstrate love and caring, because it does not come naturally to them. This is especially true for Alpha Centaurian men – they have to learn that, here on Planet Earth, this is how we show emotion, through the things we do and say.

Some never bother to learn the emotional aspect though.

What you will see most often is that Alpha Centaurians show love through practical acts of service. They will do for others what they perceive "needs" to be done, and to them there is no better way of showing their love for someone – doing something of practical use. Not surprisingly, this means their efforts are not always valued and seen for what they are! Many misunderstandings can come from this.

So, to summarize, Alpha Centaurians have an unwavering connection to Source energy and have an innate sense of the soul being free and fearless, and immortal. Practical, protective and steadfast they can have a level of self-sufficiency which in itself can lead to not asking for help from others and seeming like they are sufficient unto themselves.

Dysfunctional

The dysfunctional aspect of this Soul Group is disconnection, and this comes in when the self-containment and self-sufficiency start to be taken towards the extreme.

Some Alpha Centaurians can become real hermits and loners who make no effort to engage or understand their emotional body and do not relate to others well. Sometimes this disconnection has a "practical" twist. For example, an Alpha Centaurian may become a workaholic, and will tell himself that he is providing for his family and doing it for them, when in reality, he simply cannot connect to them and is using work to hide from this fact.

Alpha Centaurian women tend to struggle less with this than the men. The Alpha Centaurian has a strong provider instinct, and the less self-aware they are the more likely they are to disappear into their work and rationalise why this is ok, when the reality is they just don't want to deal with the emotions of their family or partner, or feel inadequate at this level and don't want to go there. They will also perceive their partner or family's emotions as being frustrating and irrational, so they stick to what they know!

Another aspect which can become dysfunctional is their tendency towards self-sufficiency. An Alpha Centaurian who allows this free rein means that not only will they not ask for help from others, even when it is badly needed, but there can be an aspect of not nurturing the self, not looking after the body. They can be quite aesthetic and withdraw into their shell or become a real hermit.

They need to remind themselves that we are all here, Starseed or otherwise, to experience and enjoy life in the physical body, and that whilst the connections to Source is primary, it should not lead to disconnection with others. That is not part of the mission.

Star Family - Andromeda or Mission Realmers

Mission Realmers are an interesting and unusual group of Starseeds in that they don't originate from the Milky Way galaxy, but from our nearest neighbour, the Andromeda galaxy – hence they are sometimes referred to as Andromedans.

They come from a very loving, beautiful and intelligent race of higher angelic beings living in the 12th dimensional energies. They have literally come to Earth with a 'mission' to help resolve the levels of negativity which have built up here and stand in the way of both the planet and humanity's Ascension to higher frequencies. It is, however, very difficult for them to find themselves in third dimensional incarnation. For this reason there are not many Mission Realmers who make the transition into a physical body.

They are here with the highest of ideals – to manifest heaven on earth and to resolve the problem of negativity on Earth.

Just by being here these beautiful, gentle beings help to open up new galactic energetic pathways between galaxies. Not surprisingly these gentle souls are inherently powerful but come from a space of 'beingness' not 'doingness' and can often appear to be quite passive and detached.

They have a level of non-attachment and 'being' which can mean they are not goal-focused or driven in any way, which can seem like they either don't care or can't be bothered. This is far from the truth – they are very gentle, loving and caring souls – but they need to take ownership of their human experience and take

steps to make it what it needs to be.

They came here with a mission and in third dimensional density this won't happen unless they make it so.

They can find being in the body quite difficult – a physical body is foreign to them. They have a sense of non-attachment to the material realm, including the physical body. As a result they have to take care to value and look after the physical body, which is after all the vehicle for their consciousness.

It can seem like a lot of trouble to them – exercise, good nutrition, sleep etc but they need to get to grips with this and figure out their own way of approaching things (rather than adopting someone elses methodology) so that they come to own it and commit to it.

The third dimension is very dense and they have to learn how to operate at this level. One of the things which helps to create movement within this density is emotion and desire. Coming from a healthy, egoic perspective this can help us achieve goals and tune in to the passion of our soul. If we don't feel desire for what we want we make no effort to achieve it. It literally pulls us towards it.

Mission Realmers have to learn that in 3D it is not enough to just be, they have to do also, and that the ego, used in a healthy way, can help with this. They need to find something they can care about and attach to at a healthy level otherwise it is all too easy to just float through life.

It is essential they find the motivation to set goals and learn to cultivate their sense of desire. They have wonderful gifts to give to the world and this does not happen when they sit back and do nothing. They need to get them out into the world.

This sense of passivity and live and let live is one of the Mission Realmers biggest challenges. A single Mission Realmer can work wonders due to their frequency, but only if they stir themselves to do so and put themselves out there.

To date Mission Realmers have been less than dynamic in setting out to achieve their 'mission', and are having to learn to step up into their power – which is considerable – in order to so. The ways of 12th dimensional beingness do not translate into 3D.

It is not that they need to lose themselves in the unending busyness so many people disappear into. They can be great role models in teaching us how to slow down and come back to ourselves. But they came here to help resolve negativity and they need to begin to show us more actively how this can be done.

They have a gentle, quiet presence and a quiet profile which doesn't demand attention, which can make this challenging. They will not push themselves forwards but they can radiate an incredibly powerful field when they come into alignment with their mission, which helps others 'get' what this is all about.

Their presence in and of itself has a healing quality and they carry this gift with them wherever they go and whatever they do. They have a beautiful peaceful and soothing energy and have a great deal of spirutal wisdom and insight they can share. Mission Realmers are excellent listeners and easily hold space for others, being non-judgemental and detached and never come from a place of egoic attachment.

They are naturally quite psychic and have a strong intuition, which they may not acknowledge. Mission Realmers need to learn to trust and use this sixth sense to navigate through the 3D realm.

It is not unusual to find a Mission Realmer who may be embracing a different type of lifestyle or relationship on Earth. They can find some of Earth systems very challenging and you will not find them willingly working within any of the corrupt systems of politics, healthcare, business etc. This is anathema to them. Individualism is important to them as is integrity.

Dysfunctional

Victimisation can become the dysfunctional aspect of these gentle, loving souls. They often incarnate into difficult and negative family situations or take on negative relationships. This is because they are seeking to transform these, not understanding that some souls are very happy with the negative choices they have made and that they are not looking to change their consciousness. They are very happy where they are thank you!

So they stay in these dysfunctional relationships, feeding ever more energy into them in an attempt to shift the negativity, and end up vastly depleted without having achieved anything. As they are not very assertive they can be easily pushed around and abused.

Rather than keep feeding energy to a negative soul, they need to use the skills they have to discern if there is first a willingness to change and focus their efforts where they will do most good.

It is also easy for a Mission Realmer to find themselves on the wrong kind of life path because they do not make the effort to exert themselves in this respect, being easily led by their family's expectations of them, rather than following their own emotional and spiritual fulfilment. It is not unknown for a Mission Realmer to end up in military service due to not exerting themselves which is the height of abuse for these gentle souls.

It can be hard to let go of draining relationships or enforcing a little tough love, but the depletion can be such that chronic health issues start to come into play. This then becomes the double whammy of not only being drained of energy by a negative soul but also inhabiting a physical body which is in pain. As a result the instinct is to detach further from physicality rather than embracing it.

Star Family - Appollonia

This is one of the newer star races to be identified on Earth and there is still confusion around exactly where their home star is – some say it is an as yet unidentified twin star of Alcyone in the Pleiades and others that it is a star in the Alpha Centauri constellation.

No doubt this confusion will be sorted out in time – we should just be grateful Appollonians are bringing their talents here at this time to help Earth and her inhabitants through these difficult and challenging times.

Appollonians are curious and love learning – they are like sponges soaking up all information no matter how eclectic it is. They are the original life-long learners and will not limit themselves to a single speciality.

As a result they hate being labelled or limited. They resist being pigeon-holed and tightly defined, and are very free spirits. Normally calm and cool, if they feel someone is trying to confine or limit them in any way it is likely to get a strong reaction.

They are sensitive and empathic souls and if they chose make good healers, particularly of mental and emotional pain, as they can help others release this. They also have a deep connection the Earth and nature and an Appollonian Starseed will easily and quickly connect into earth energies, nature spirits and other interdimensional beings and may therefore follow a

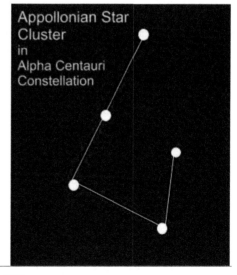

Appollonian Star Cluster in Alpha Centauri Constellation

healing path for the planet, animals and human beings.

They are self-reliant and independent souls and avoid wherever possible depending on others in any way – emotionally, financially etc. They can also be somewhat serious-minded and maybe need to remind themselves on occasion to lighten up and enjoy the experience of being on Earth a little more, have a little fun!

Being in nature will be very healing and balancing for these beautiful souls.

Soul Family - Arcturus

Arcturus is the brightest star in the Boötes constellation, and the brightest star in the northern celestial hemisphere (fourth brightest planet overall). It is an ageing star, around 2 ½ billion years older than Earth's sun.

It is rare for Arcturians to incarnate into full physicality. Their system resonates within the 7th dimension, whilst Earth is the 3rd dimension. Quite a difference! And therefore full physicality is not first choice for most Arcturians. It is more likely that you will meet them inter-dimensionally as spirit guides, helpers and teachers.

The few who do choose to fully incarnate in a human body are highly spiritual and will be very involved or interested in areas of spirituality, metaphysics and esoteric lore.

Highly conscious, spiritual and intuitive individuals they uphold spiritual wisdom and have a great deal of insight to share with others. As a soul group they have a strong desire to be of service to the Collective.

They do not, however, aspire to be well-known, famous or in the public eye. They are quiet individuals who prefer to remain in the background. They are often the influencers behind the influencers, the people who know everyone but that no-one has ever heard of. They quietly share their insight and wisdom with those who have high profiles and influence events at this level.

Arctureans are somewhat baffled by existing social structures and systems that don't seem to "make sense" to them. They don't understand why

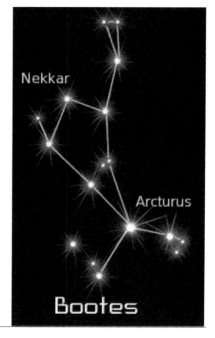

humanity so often chooses chaos and unfairness instead of balance and order. They also will have difficulty around individuals or groups who chose to behave in this way also – why would you deliberately chose dramas and irrationality?

Like so many Starseeds who have incarnated into human bodies, this aspect of being a human being completely baffles them. It is often at times like this that the first inkling of difference starts to penetrate through the 'forgetting' intrinsic to 3D incarnation.

Arcturians are also likely to reject participating in social structures which don't make sense to them – marriage, religion, even educational establishments. When forced to participate – as children are with education – they will often just not engage. Social manipulation or guilt trips won't work on them either. They see it for what it is and will turn their back on it.

They are highly intelligent, as well as being sensitive. They have an affinity with advanced technologies, science, computing, astronomy, mathematics etc. and will be working behind the scenes to bring new, better ways of using technology, producing energy etc to the planet.

Arcturians are also known to be gifted healers, particularly at the energetic level, although they might also be found trying to bring reform to the worst practices and misunderstandings of mainstream medicine.

Coming from a 7D perspective, they have an innate understanding of the geometries of light and energy and how this underpins healing and how we need to apply this to new technologies, mathematics, architecture and so on in a way which is in tune with natural laws rather than breaking them to the detriment of the Planet.

When something defies common sense they don't get it, and may reject that social or corporate structure that demands nonsensical adherence to harmful or inappropriate practices.

Sensitive, loving and peaceful Arcturians know the value of little acts of everyday kindness. To those who don't know them they can appear mysterious or aloof as they are cautious who they let into their personal space and inner circle. Their sensitivity to energy means they are selective about who they let in close to them.

Most Arcturians will find themselves drawn to the high vibrational frequencies of crystals and gemstones, as well as symbols and sigils which have a language of their own.

Most Arcturians have to beware of being ungrounded. They are naturally very comfortable in the higher dimensions and with higher frequencies, and can have an imbalance with too much energy in their higher chakras. This can lead to grounding being a challenge to them, and they may find the everyday physical tasks of keeping body and soul together – cooking, cleaning, eating etc – tedious and difficult to engage with.

Not looking after the body properly can be a problem, as can gaining weight in order to ground themselves better. Regular, daily grounding practices can serve them much better.

Dysfunctional

There is the potential for every group to fall into dysfunctional patterns and Arcturians are no exception. The dysfunctional aspect of this soul family can be their tendency to go into secret rebellion against "normal" social structures which they don't agree with or want to engage with, rather than openly seeking to challenge and reform them. They turn their back rather than try to bring about change for the greater good of all.

A healthy way of doing this would see them, in their own quiet way, coming out very honestly with their opinions and say 'this conflicts with Universal wisdom, this needs changing'. They can then become an advocate for change in a very sensible mature and helpful way, without lots of drama. This is where Arcturians can be a great asset.

But if they don't feel safe enough, or trust enough to do this they can instead just turn their back on things and go into a secret, silent rebellion where they won't engage and won't have dialogue around it and will often do things behind the scenes that are inappropriate, can be hurtful to others or are often acts of self-sabotage in order to make a (silent) point – a classic cut off one's nose to spite one's face type of scenario.

So they don't learn to express what they disagree with, they keep it to themselves and behave in a way which isn't helpful.

Often Arctureans may start having "secret lives" that allow them to express aspects of themselves that don't feel able to express openly as it doesn't quite fit into society's perception of "normal," rather than taking a stand for living the Truth of who they are.

This is a shame as the high vibration they can bring to an issue when it is handled well can bring about the right kind of change, benefiting others who feel like them. It holds the potential for conflict though, and Arcturians hate this as much as they hate the spotlight.

They need to be open and honest and taking a stand at least with the people they know though, so they don't end up living a lie and compromising themselves. In addition there is always the potential of showing others a different way of behaving that works and they can change people's minds. They have so much insight and wisdom to share it is a shame when they chose to keep it to themselves.

As a Collective we need their insight and wisdom, and when they keep it to themselves no one benefits. They therefore don't serve anyone and can end up instead sabotaging themselves and their relationships.

Star Family - Cassiopeia

Cassiopeia, the Queen, is a constellation in the northern sky which revolves around Polaris, the North Star.

It is named after a queen from Greek mythology who boasted that her daughter was more beautiful than the sea nymphs, the Nereids, causing the sea god Poseidon to send a sea monster to ravage the kingdom. Her daughter, Andromeda, was offering up in sacrifice to the monster, but rescued by the hero Perseus in the nick of time!

Not that this myth really has anything to do with the beings from this star system. They are very high dimensional, and are imbued with the frequency of the Divine Feminine and unconditional love.

Their frequency is such that they live in their light bodies, so coming into physicality is like wearing a heavy suit of armour – as it is for all high frequency beings. As a race within the galaxy they are fighters for Peace, or maybe it is better to say they are champions for peace, as peace is never gained by fighting.

As Starseeds here on Earth they embody this love for justice, equality, harmony and balance and are wonderfully loving and kind people. Not many Cassiopeians incarnate physically, most who are helping Earth are part of the great group of interdimensional, intergalactic beings helping from off-planet. They chose to have a few 'insiders' through whom they would incarnate, and they could

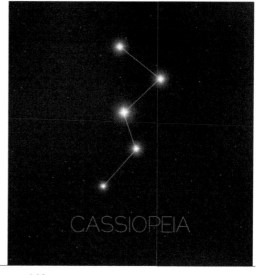

communicate with through dreams or trance to encourage certain actions to be taken.

Cassiopeians are excellent strategic planners, organisers and communicators, empathic and compassionate. They will usually be found in humanitarian or sociological areas helping others and trying to bring about changes for the better.

The loving frequency of the Cassiopeian shines through them and attracts those who can find great healing and acceptance in this energy.

Optimistic and outgoing, they bring beauty into their environment in whatever way possible – art, architecture, nature, interior design or whatever way they can, as beauty carries a frequency which expands the human heart.

Star Family - Cygnus

Cygnus is a constellation in the Northern sky which contains one of the brightest stars in the night sky – Deneb. It is also sometimes called the Northern Cross. Cygnus is Latin for swan.

Very few Starseeds from Cygnus ever come into incarnation on Earth. The few who do are here to learn. They are the ones you might find at a social gathering hanging back and taking it all in. They are good listeners rather than talkers, absorbing information which is filed away.

They may appear to be detached and not really care as they are not very expressive by nature, but family and friends are important to them. Often the depth of their emotions may be glimpsed in any artistic endeavours they undertake. They have a strong sense of duty and tend to be very punctual.

They are not into 'stuff' for its own sake. They look for quality rather than quantity, have good taste, do not make impulse buys or splurge unnecessarily, thinking any decision through carefully and are generally very patient by nature.

All this, together with their sense of duty and work ethic can make them at first glance seem rather boring, but they have great depths which become obvious to those who take time to know them better.

Cygnian culture is technically advanced and has a high level of comfort. Cygnian Starseeds seek that same level of comfort in life here on Earth, and embrace – and improve – Earth technology, thriving around gadgets, electronics and technology of all kind.

Beyond this, very little more is known at the current time, as so few Cygnians chose to come into Earth incarnation.

Star Family - Draco

Draconian souls are from the constellation of Draco. Draco is Latin for dragon, and this constellation is made up from quite a number of stars which are home to a variety of both reptiloid and winged draconic races.

The Draconians themselves say they originally came into this universe from another many billions of years ago and settled in the Draco region. They tell this as part of their race history, but the understood history of this Universe would seem to contradict this. Who is right? Impossible to say, but it lends itself to the narrative from the negative Draconian races that this is 'their' Universe.

There is much written about the 'negative' impact of Draconian races, but in truth there would seem to be at least two, probably more, separate races – the extremely militant, dominant and aggressive races source from the Fallen Omicron Dragon-Moth lineage and the Fallen Odedicron Reptilian lineage (neither of these are to be confused with the Fallen reptilian Anunnaki races which come from another lineage altogether). It can be confusing and here is not the place to expand on the fallen Draconian races.

Suffice it to say that there are very highly evolved Draconians also who are working from a different level of consciousness altogether, very heart-centred and highly evolved. Unfortunately, all too often they get lumped together with the fallen races from this sector of the galaxy

Draco

(who are rightly feared and have wreak havoc wherever they go).

The legacy of this on Earth has impacted heavily on the negative perception of Draconians – and indeed dragons – in the Western hemisphere. In the East where any interaction was often with the more evolved representatives of Draco there is a very benevolent and positive attitude towards dragons.

The positive Draconian races are well aware of the bad rap they have been tainted with here on Earth and tend to keep in the background, aiding from afar.

Positive Draconians, along with many other star races are all engaged in supporting and enabling where possible the raising of consciousness on Earth, and whilst it is easy to focus on the negative side they would not be spiritually evolved enough to be part of the Starseed missions to Earth. Just let it be said that if you come across a negative Draconian soul they will be recognisable as they are energy 'drains', leaching energy from other beings and 'feeding' off strong emotions of fear or upset which they have often promulgated through aggression, manipulation, disempowerment and control. They are warmongers, very hierarchical, authoritarian and totally serve their own agenda.

They are part of the matrix which tries to convince humanity of the need for suffering, sacrifice, hierarchy and the need to follow elitist authorities without question, even if it means acting against your own Divine nature.

Positive Draconian souls who have chosen to come into incarnation to help the evolving consciousness on Earth are powerful beings, with a strong desire to bring order out of chaos and help awaken an understanding of unconditional love on the planet. They can be very heart-centred.

There can often be a tough exterior, and a guarded and wary nature with all those not in their inner circle, but it hides a heart of gold, and they seek to transcend differences and are very accepting of all walks of life. They have a very protective attitude to the planet and its people, and if you have a Draconian Starseed friend or partner they will be fiercely loyal and protective.

Draconians do not tend to have any well-developed psychic sense but they do have an extremely well-developed instinctual sense which serves them well.

They have a profound sense of loyalty and duty towards helping humanity evolve, partly in recompense for what happened back in Earth's history that has been the cause of so much darkness and suffering, but also because there is an innate nobility to the benevolent dragon. They rightly have a reputation for great wisdom also, so whilst they may not have much to say – they are often not the most chatty of people – when they do speak it can be worth listening carefully to what they say.

They make excellent leaders, co-ordinators and organisers and behind the somewhat gruff or detached exterior are willing to help anyone along the way to achieving their potential. They have excellent skills in leading, organising, structuring and building something and have access to deep wisdom when centred and aligned.

A positive Draconian soul is a powerful and loyal force for good on the planet and should not be confused with the negative races. They can sometimes come over as wary and aloof, even arrogant, and guard their heart energy, but if you can persuade a positive Draconian soul to open up you are indeed lucky as you are enveloped in their warmth and love and protection.

Star Family – Earther

Earth is your home world. This is the only world an Earther knows as a Soul, they have not had any incarnations elsewhere in the galaxy, but were born in on their soul frequency to this planet.

Generally Earthers are much younger souls than Starseeds, but when it comes to this planet they are well versed in what it means to be living in physicality, they know how to live and operate here.

Earth is a unique experiment within the Universe. The Earth Blueprint is based on creating through physical, mental, emotional and spiritual realms *simultaneously.* The human blueprint, to come into its full potential requires mastery of these realms, work in co-creation with universal consciousness. Human DNA and its Divine Blueprint is an advanced blueprint when it is fully activated.

When open to Universal Consciousness and Light the human form and its genetic template can enable multidimensional creation. No wonder so many come here seeking mastery of physicality and the emotional and mental realms.

Choosing to birth into dense matter, we are all Spirit having a physical experience – and the Earth plane is the place *par excellence* to gain this experience, as here you are not just part of a Collective, but also an individual soul expressing itself through this Collective.

There is an abundance of life and life forms on Earth and the Earthers' soul purpose is to create the experience of life on this planet in all its facets, and to experience what it is to live from each of the realms – physical, mental, emotional, spiritual and evolve its template to enable interdimensional travel whilst in form. This is unique to Earth.

Unfortunately, there has been a lot of deliberate interference in the evolution of this template by those who have negative intentions towards humanity. They have cause many problems, including the memory-wiping and amnesia which coming into physicality on the Earth in recent millennia has entailed. As a consequence separation and forgetting they are part of a galactic family is a major problem for all Earth souls at present.

As a result most decisions and choices on Earth are made from fear and separation, not from the Light, and many Starseeds are here to help correct this at this time.

Earthers have a deep commitment to Mother Earth, and reincarnate here again and again. They are here to help unfold the Divine Blueprint for Life on Earth, and have a guardianship role to seed life and give life creative expression here as well as witnessing the beauty of physical creation all around.

Earthers are not here for physical aggression and gaining power over others, but this is what the experience of separation and infiltration by negative aliens has bought in, as the desire for connection wrought by separation has led most to looking outside themselves for connection rather than to Source, and to giving their power away in order to 'belong'.

In addition, awakened Earthers are Guardians of the Earth Consciousness Grids and Stargates – but few, if any, are currently functioning at this level.

For all of us, Earther or Starseed, it is important to listen to your own Truth, and not to the agendas of others. Earthers signed up to experience life through the unification of mind, spirit and physical body, and to experience life through the five senses, as well as gain mastery over the emotional, mental and spiritual aspects of being.

Earther Souls are grounded, practical individuals who are very comfortable living within the physical experience – they should be as this is their home planet! Earthers are here living Life – their purpose is that simple; To give creative expression to Life and to bear witness to its great beauty.

The primary goal of most Earthers is comfort, safety and security – and why wouldn't it be! They have had many lifetimes on this planet when life was anything but this, so there is a deep desire for security. Many hold within them great trauma from past catastrophes and wars which needs to be cleared for them to access back to the original intent of choosing this as their planet of birth.

Earthers have a strong relationship with this planet and may be interested in Earth healing energies such as crystal healing, shamanic work etc.

They also, not surprisingly, have a concern for the environment, Nature, and living creatures. They are dedicated to this world's welfare – or at least those who haven't gone astray and got lost in the power plays and polarities of separation and duality are!

They also have a strong connection with nature and its wellbeing - being outside is balancing and important to them. Enjoying life to the full through exploring the richness and sensuality of the five senses, as well as through the emotional body, and mental and spiritual dimensions is something they came here to do.

Choosing to be born an Earther is about a soul exploring life, enjoying life, experiencing life in all its multiple forms and facets.

As has been stated, separation can be an issue for them. As beings who chose to come here from the start there was a choice to participate in some degree with separation from Source Energy as physicality is a dense frequency and of necessity involves coming away from the lighter, higher frequencies. This sense of loss is felt, albeit often unconsciously, and very often leads to looking outside oneself for connection in a vain effort to re-connect to Source energy.

So they seek others to either make them feel whole through relationships (which never works as a strategy) or they seek spiritual connection through the promises held out by others such as religions or belonging to various groups or tribal entities.

Of course, the only way Earthers will re-connect to the Creator energy is by going within and discovering their Spiritual origins and beginning the journey of the soul back home.

Dysfunctional

There is always the potential for dysfunctionality within any group. The dysfunctional aspect of this Soul Group is complacency. They may become overly focused on physical comfort and safety to the point of stagnation.

Ultimately they need to remember they are Spirit having a physical experience and come back to the challenge of this.

Typical Earther souls go to work, doing a job they maybe don't love but don't hate, come home, eat dinner, have a beer with friends, watch TV, go to bed ...and then do it all again, the next day....and the next....and the next...

Why?

Because it gives a sense of safety and security! They don't like getting out of their comfort zone because they are wired for comfort.

This is, of course, largely illusory and is part of the paradigm of separation that it is required to break out of.

They like to uphold a sense of tradition and stability, of roots, for this same reason, which in itself is not a problem, but some spontaneity and freshness needs to be introduced to leaven the potential staleness of always doing things the same way.

Earthers are really how we define 'normal' on our planet – and they make up the majority of souls here, who have signed up to be part of the great Earth experiment of gaining mastery of living through the physical, mental, emotional and spiritual realms simultaneously. Ultimately the Earth Blueprint calls for the great diversity of life here to work in harmony across all the realms and all beings – Unity in Diversity is the aim.

Star Family - Eridanus

This star system has been known as an Elven star system called the 'River in the Sky' and is one of the largest constellations in the heavens.

Mythically it is linked to the ancient city of Eridu, sacred to the god Enki-Ea, ruler of the Abyss and the waters. It is also linked to the myth of Phaeton whose father was the sun god and after much pestering from his son allowed him the reins of the sun chariot. Unable to control it, it veered wildly about, scorching both heaven and earth until the King of the Gods, Zeus, struck him dead with a thunderbolt and he fell to Earth. The constellation is supposed to trace his wildly veering path.

The inhabited twin sun stars of Epsilon Eridani and Isilari Eridani are said to be inhabited by an Elven race of what we would call great magic and power. The Elven races played an early role in the seeding of Earth and have a keen interest in what is unfolding now.

It is said that Eridanians, coming from a high level of consciousness, in order to incarnate on Earth, seeded particular bloodlines that would have the necessary capacity to hold their level of consciousness, which has given rise to all sorts of stories of elite bloodlines families quietly shepherding Earth civilization from behind the scenes for the last few millennia. True or not? At this moment it is impossible to say.

What we do know is that the negative alien beings who have caused such havoc here on Earth are known to have hunted down and massacred

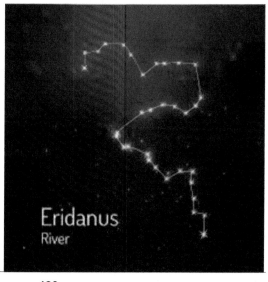

Eridanus
River

certain human bloodlines at various points in our not so distant history. Are some of these the Elven races who, legend says, disappeared in the 'hollow hills' (dimensions?) to escape to safety?

If there are Eridanian Starseeds incarnating today through these same bloodlines, little is known about them beyond the fact they have great inner and outer strength, are quick-thinking, intuitive, free spirited, smart, loyal, adventurous and usually involved in the esoteric, magical, metaphysical areas of knowledge and have an 'old soul' quality about them.

The strength and wisdom – and magical abilities – of the Elven race is recorded in various mythologies, and this hints at certain advanced lineages of Star Beings that are the progenitors, with others, of the human race.

Star Family - Hadar

The planet Hadar is within the star system of Beta Centauri, and close neighbours to the Alpha Centaurians.

Hadar is known throughout the Universe to be the planet of Divine Love.

For eons Hadar has been the planetary container or Love and it stood as a beacon within the Universe as such. It is only relatively recently that Hadarians have started to take this frequency out into the cosmos to others where it is badly needed.

Love is the universal governing frequency and is foundational to the Earth Blueprint, which has become badly distorted. Hadarians incarnating here on Earth come in service to humanity to help remind us of this frequency and bring us back to it.

Love permeates everything as a heart connection which opens us to beauty, grace, abundance and joy. It asks us to both share and BE Love and Hadarians have always understood this and come from this place. The collective expression of Love is known to Hadarian souls and it is quite simply the only way there is according to Hadarian souls.

This has led in their past to some unhappy history with other Beings in the Universe who made the choice long ago to choose darkness as their power source. These Beings came from the constellation of Draco, which is one of the largest constellations in the sky and made up of many star systems.

This has unfortunately given all Draconians a bad name.

As Hadarians had no concept of making choices from anything less than Love, this naivety enabled the negative Draconians to enslave the Hadarians in an attempt to possess their Light. The Universe does not allow this, it is against natural law. Every soul connects to Love through connection to Source.

We are all Divine sparks of the Creator and we hold that connection within. Effectively tapping into and trying to steal another's Light energy is forbidden. Taking the Divine Love collectively emanated by the Hadarians was a serious breech and other star races came to their aid, freeing them from their enslavement. But the trauma left an imprint on many Hadarian souls.

Those brave Hadarian souls who choose to keep incarnating on Earth can easily have this trauma re-awakened within them by the many energy vampires and negative beings who prey on the Light energy of Earth. In some respects the same battle is being fought, only this time it is for Earth's Light. Darkness and negativity will never win in a Universe founded on Love, but it can do great damage.

It is not unusual for Hadarians to have difficulty with relationships here, due to the transactional nature of relationships on Earth. Even romantic relationships work at this level and it can be a shock as to how transactional everything is.

Hadarians have come to bring an understanding of the unconditional nature of Love and that the frequency of Love is the primary frequency of the Cosmos. They are here to help re-activate and inspire this to be the governing frequency for Earth. Unfortunately there are those quite content to let them do all the heavy lifting at this level, whilst they enjoy the benefits without giving anything back.

Equally, there can be an intensity to the way a Hadarian loves that can be quite scary to others. And Hadarians can be dissatisfied in the way they are loved in return – it will not be unconditional as that is not the nature of relationships here on our planet, so there will inevitably be disappointment.

A Hadarian soul needs to learn to become discerning and slightly conditional around the Love they emanate. They are souls who bring a pure expression of unconditional love into any relationship they have, and that is so easily abused by those of less than pure intent. Often they find themselves in friendships and relationships where others take all they have to give, but offer little in return.

Tough Love is not natural to Hadarians, but this is what they need to bring to these situations, rather than even more Love, which is their default, to change things for the better. Some relationships are worth saving and some are not and learning to use judgment in these matters is part of the learning Hadarians have here on Earth.

At the moment on Earth unconditional Love is only possible in relationship to the Self, and they need to bear this in mind, and look after their own well-being first. All other Earth relationships have some degree of conditionality to them and if a Hadarian persists with a relationship which is not equal a sense of victimhood can ensue.

Indeed Hadarians have been over-represented in past incarnations in those who have been abused, victimised and taken advantage of. Not surprisingly, therefore, it is common for Hadarians who have a history here to fear being taken advantage of and this is soul memory harking back to the time in Hadar's history when the Hadarian Light of Love was similarly abused. Reconnecting to the Divine and re-igniting the Light of the Divine within can help alleviate this.

Hadarians who hold a sense of victimhood or deep sadness and disconnection to the world can bring themselves back into balance by journeying back to their home world, and reconnecting to the frequencies of Love and Light held there. Establishing this connection and keeping it strong can help them cope with the heavier energies of Earth.

The Hadarian home world is a place of unconditional love, the energy that Hadarian Souls bring to our planet today to remind and inspire us. They are incredibly loving souls and help us to value the individual gifts we all hold. They see individuation as the appreciation and respect for the unique spark of the Divine found within everyone, and the unique expression and gifts it brings to the world. They see everyone as being the individual facet of a beautiful and brilliant diamond. Each fact is integral to the beauty of the whole, lending its fire and beauty to the Collective expression of this, whilst being unique in itself.

To a Hadarian Soul, there is beauty in everything. It is all to be enjoyed and respected and experienced with wonder and pleasure. They are playful and creative souls who have immense fun weaving together the endless possibilities for how to express Love in all they do and are. Fun and spontaneous, their generous natures will invite you along for the ride if you want to come. If you do – great! If you don't, that's great also!

Hadarians thrive best in a situation where there is quick feedback and gratification. Expecting them to thrive working on projects which give long term results or payback does not work for them, and will leave them feeling dissatisfied and unappreciated.

Hadarians feel deeply the free-will choices made at a collective level which have taken humanity away from the frequency of Love. They see the coming Shift as a huge opportunity to get things back on track, and are here working with many other Starseeds to ensure this opportunity is not missed.

With a choice made from a frequency other than Love not only is the door opened to fear but without Love there is no communion with nature, higher mind, spirit, other Light beings etc. Hadarians see this as a void within each of us. Rather than feel the pain of this, if a Hadarian can breathe love into the space they can gently help to fill the gaps.

It is a challenge for Hadarians to be so sensitive here in 3rd dimensionality, and yet they hold within their memory banks the essence of Love – all they need to do in order to draw on this is to remember and radiate this remembrance through into every situation.

They have known a glorious existence prior to being here. Compared to where they have come from, it can seem to Hadarians that they have been plunged into the pits of Hell, but they are loving and positive souls and if they can keep their Light strong they can bring the change so sorely needed.

Re-establishing the umbilical cord back to the higher frequencies that birthed them can be a lifeline to them, nourishing and supporting them in their mission here.

Hadarians are often very interested in experimenting with what looks like very unconventional relationships, such as polyamory, open relationships, communal living and so on, as they play with the many ways love can be expressed. The kind of taboos that many societies bring to anything outside a strict window of behaviour feels very repressive and leaves many Hadarians feeling misplaced here on our planet. They might be quite restless souls as they look for 'home', but there is nowhere else on this planet that will make them feel more complete, so they need to bear this in mind.

A Hadarian quirk is that they often have the ability to let time work for them – they can gently play with the concept of time and stretch it or contract it as required.

Dysfunctional

Any dysfunctionality in this soul group – and it can be quite rare as they are high frequency souls – will be due to the soul yearning for the unconditional love that they knew and was the norm on their home planet.

If this gets out of hand they can become manipulative in order to try and get the love they seek, maybe self-sabotaging in order to 'make' someone come riding to the rescue, or becoming co-dependent in relationship, blurring the boundaries between themselves and others.

Journeying back to their home planet and re-establishing the connection to this Love as already described can be of immense help to a starseed Hadarian.

Star Family - Hyades

The Hyades is a star cluster to be found in the head of the constellation of Taurus the Bull. It forms a distinctive 'V' or arrow shape, with the brightest star, Aldebran, also forming the eye of the Bull.

I understand that this cluster was populated by refugees fleeing the great galactic conflict between the reptilian races and those of Lyra eons back in galactic history.

Wise, gentle, loving, compassionate they are known to never give up on anyone, no matter what. They see the spark of the Divine in even the darkest of characters and will work to grown this tiny spark into a greater light.

Their empathy for others and ability to see the other's point of view, to walk in their shoes, means their sensitive nature is often hurt, but their loving and loyal nature can give them a very long piece of elastic.

They have been part of the galactic forces guiding Earth and her civilisations behind the scenes for eons, but are generally not as well known or visible as other races such as the Pleidians or Arcturians.

The Hyades cluster

Star Family - Indigo Races

The Indigo Races are interesting as we are not so much talking about a specific planet of origin here – Indigos show up in various planetary systems and in various dimensions. Rather what defines an Indigo is actually their DNA template rather than a specific point of origin and how much of it is already activated on birthing here on Earth.

The human DNA template has a 12-strand potentiality, most of which is dormant. Most people on the Earth, due to digression, deliberate manipulation, tampering and other nefarious activities, have only 2 or 3 strands of this template activated, with the result that the human race is a species with amnesia, making it victim to manipulation and control measures deliberately implemented to prevent it from reclaiming the fullness of its DNA legacy.

This is part of a story that goes back to the beginning of human history and is for another time, but it has led to the need for those galactic and interdimensional races with the 12-strand and above template to intervene here on Earth at this time in order to enable those who are wishing to be part of the Shift or Ascension process that we are currently

moving through to do so. Without their help it is unlikely most of humanity would make it.

Indigos are part of this intervention force, a type of lightworker who have come together to be of aid at this time.

Indigos are birthed on this planet with the 6th dimensional frequency band of consciousness (the 6th DNA strand) already activated. Not only does this give them quick access to information and frequencies as they grow up, but also gives them the Indigo colour spectrum of frequency in their auric field.

The Indigos are here to hold the higher frequency of their activated template within the planetary field and grids helping to bring in the light codes required to activate and stabilise them, and heal the immense damage perpetrated on the consciousness grids by negative intervention.

There is another purpose that this group has and that is as what are called Agents of Transformation – the system busters and harbingers of a new way of doing things within the societies on this planet. It is the awakened and activated Indigos who are helping to bring in some of the vast much-needed changes we are beginning to see across the global systems of our societies – a new way of understanding ourselves, of understanding community and individuality, of finance, of connection to nature and all life on the planet, of healthcare etc.

Many are energy placement holders, preparing for a certain marker point and energetic opening up to begin their mission.

Their Collective soul mission is to help Earth and humanity at this time raise sufficient frequency to be able to ascend during this Stellar Activation Ascension Cycle[6] we are currently moving through, and to move out of the old paradigms of control, manipulation, greed,

---

[6] A Stellar Activation Cycle happens approximately every 26,000 years and is a period when the Universal Stargates on Earth open naturally and Earth and all her beings have a chance to move an entire dimensional field up an octave.

enslavement and fear which have dominated this planet during this last dark cycle.

In many ways they are the greatest hope humanity has of escaping from the disastrous interference and manipulation of various Fallen races that have resulted in the current mess we find ourselves in.

But….

Indigos, just like the rest of us, are subject to the planetary amnesia that affects almost every soul who descends into incarnation here, due to the heavy mind wiping programmes that have been installed.

Much work is going on off-planet to find and dismantle these mechanisms, but in the meantime the activated Indigo template ensures many of them are 'remembering' their purpose and mission from an early age.

As a result they are very special children, who began incarnating here in large numbers during the 1980s and 1990s, although there has been an advance guard of Indigos incarnating here for the last 100 years or so to help prepare the way for the main influx – a tough mission in an unawakened world!

The Fallen races have not taken this influx of high frequency souls to the planet lying down, as the Indigos can, and are, upsetting all their very carefully laid plans. As a result many Indigos, even today, are being taken down very effectively with the toxic mix of pharmaceutical vaccines and drugs early on, an education system that refuses to acknowledge their uniqueness and labels them disruptive, difficult etc and often drugs them into compliance, and a corporate world that is very unsympathetic of their desire to work cooperatively, Collectively and for the good of all.

Many Indigos have been deeply wounded and even foundered on the rocks thrown in their way, but the sheer weight of numbers and the increasing frequency of those coming in is beginning to bring in the paradigm shift. Think of the difference between the 1960s and 1970s and today. Yes, things seem chaotic at the moment, but the green shoots of something better can be glimpsed, and this will only grow.

The Indigos are here to create change and have a keen sense of what works and what doesn't, so are well tuned to where our current systems of governance and business etc no longer serve – if they ever did! This awareness often comes in at an early age, and can cause frustration because they are too young to do much about it. They are a disruptive influence and can earn the label trouble-maker early on in school where they are a round peg the education system tries to force into a square hole.

The Indigo child doesn't take to authority well. The idea of living in a system of absolutes without question is what they're here to change. They're often isolationist, headstrong and have an in-built desire to help the world in any way they can.

They are also sensitive, often with well-developed psychic senses, highly intuitive, strong-willed and innovative. With the right parenting they can, and do achieve, from an early age – just not in full alignment with the existing paradigm. They are showing us different ways of doing just about everything.

With the 'wrong' kind of parent who is unawake and unaware they will simply be labelled destructive and obstructive, and their road will be much harder. But many do still win through.

There was a big awakening of Indigos triggered around 2007, and as more waves are incarnated in their presence is growing on the planet. All Indigos are born with distortions to the DNA and what are called Fire Letter sequences within the DNA, just as all souls who incarnate here are – they are inherited from the foetal body and parents during Foetal

Integration[7], and these must be cleared in order for Indigos to fulfil their potential. Indigos have 'stuff' to clear just as much as the rest of us.

Crystal Children

The Crystal children are the continuation of the Indigo star child lineage. They often come in as the offspring to Indigo adults as a newly incarnating soul arriving on Earth and have the activated 6th dimensional template and carry a minimum of a 12-strand DNA potential, with some carrying the 24 or even 36-strand potential. This enables them to hold a very high frequency when required.

Their characteristics are very much in line with other Indigos. Material possessions do not interest them. Neither does anything remotely superficial. They're here to make a positive contribution to the world. These souls started coming in around the turn of the millennium. They're known for having a penetrating gaze and give off a loving vibration that knows no boundaries. Crystals are most often drawn to take up positions as healers, carers, volunteers and teachers of all descriptions.

Rainbow Children

The Rainbow children were born around the year 2010 onwards. They're the latest generation of souls to come in and help humanity shift its awareness to a higher state of consciousness. All Indigos are powerful beings in their own right, but the Rainbow Children, in particular, are exceptionally talented from an early age- even by Starseed standards. You can often see stories in the media of children of no more than ten years old winning prestigious physics prizes, coming with solutions to rid the ocean of plastics or create clean water for rural villages in deprived

---

[7] Foetal integration – the process of a soul consciousness integrating into a foetus before birth. At this present time due to energetic reversal frequency NETs which cloak the planet no soul birthed here escapes some damage and memory-wiping.

countries. But this only scratches the surface of their abilities. They're special souls, and their character is beyond reproach.

Indigo Types

It is worth noting that there are different types of templating in the Indigos. Laid out below are the three major types that have been identified, with a fourth emerging.

Indigo Type 1

Type 1s are very attuned to the planetary grids[8] and the planetary fields and as such, once awakened, are generally experts in working with the larger matrices of the planetary energy fields. At this particular time, in the middle of a Stellar Activation Cycle, frequencies of energy are at times literally pouring into the grids and Indigos can transmit energy, frequency or light codes to help stabilise this incoming energy and rebalance certain planetary vortices or key nodes.

Indigo 1s will seek to bring groups of people together at key sites during these cycles of incoming energy, working with ley lines, sacred sites, vortices and stargate locations.

Individual Indigos will hold specific incarnation demographics, blood land ties and mission-based frequency activations that will be triggered at specific points when they will respond to the urge to go to a particular place at a specific time, carrying their unique light codes and embedding them within the grids, transmitting them through their energy fields.

---

[8] This refers to the grids of leylines, energy lines, portal points and natural energetic grid systems that are both on, in and above the Earth. They are often described as being an energetic equivalent of our circulation system. They hold the consciousness fields of the planet, and human consciousness is deeply connected to them. The current interference on Earth has seen many grids hijacked and artificial grids implanted which have negatively affected the consciousness of humanity. Clearing this and stabilising the new light codes into the grids is part of the Indigo mission – as it is for many lightworkers.

Some Indigos are fully conscious of what they are doing, others not. Many Indigo 1s will find themselves travelling to many countries and places for short periods of time as they respond to the nudges of their soul. Or, alternatively, they may have a contract with a particular piece of land or place.

Some of the names for the Indigo 1s are Grid keepers, Gridworkers, Grid readers, Gate keepers, Grail keeper, Land Guardians and spiritual land workers.

Indigo Type 2

Indigo Type 2s have a different kind of mission, and that is to help regenerate and activate the human DNA template potential. They will be the healers, energy workers, shamans, spiritual metaphysicians and medicine men and women.

However they work, Indigo Type 2s will work directly with the rebuilding and rehabilitation process of the DNA, helping to build the human light body and light field. Many will be bringing through new healing modalities and techniques and light codes to enable this.

The emergent understanding of the human energy field and anatomy is thanks to the waves of Indigo Type 2s incarnating in progressively larger numbers since the Second World War. It has helped to transform many people's understanding of who we are and open them up to the some of the shut-down aspects of our being.

Indigo Type 2s are the way showers for the new principles of unification and integration, as well as helping to build healing communities based on spiritual-energetic principles. They are growing our understanding of the link between our physical body and our multidimensional being and how to find balance and harmony within all of this, to enable our DNA to activate and hold ever higher levels of resonant frequency.

Indigo Type 3

Indigo Type 3s have more of a warrior role, acting as a bridge between the light and dark realms. They are the polarity integrators and probably have the most challenging role of all as they seek to integrate both aspects of this polarity.

Part of their mission is to work with the less evolved, more aggressive souls and act as role models at this level. Many are also incarnating to share space within the same body of a less evolved soul, seeking to heal the distortions within the template and integrate the two extremes of soul aspect within the bioenergy field.

Indigo Type 3s are seeking to create a template for polarity integration to heal and unify the love and fear polarities so prevalent here, enabling huge amounts of karmic patterning to be released from not just human bodies, but also the planetary body.

So you can see some of the most challenging contracts are taken on by Indigo Type 3s. They are the spiritual warriors, the alchemists, the justice fighters and master magicians, seeking to work miracles with degraded genetics and deeply damaged and fragmented genetic lineages to bring them back to a place of balance.

Indigo Type 4

This is a new type of Indigo patterning which is currently emerging which seems to be embodying all three types of Indigo patterning within themselves. These are very high frequency, carrying what is called the Double Diamond sun DNA, with a minimum of 24 strands. This enables them to carry higher galactic coding and frequencies and quickly navigate

Earth timelines, grid work and grid anatomy, and anchor cosmic codes and blueprints.

They are mental, spiritual and emotional Vision holders for the New Earth and can help to anchor these new realities into the Earth fields. They are likely to take on Guardian speaker roles, teaching the next generation of Indigos, and will pioneer new technologies that will be part of our evolutionary progression.

Dysfunctional

Like all Star Families there can be a dysfunction aspect to Indigos who have incarnated here on Earth and struggle to 'wake up' or become aware of their mission.

As has been already mentioned, they are likely within very '3D' families and institutions to be considered troublesome and difficult. Many are labelled as having ADHD or similar behavioural problems and drugged to make them compliant, others are labelled with various mental health issues and treated accordingly.

Their sensitive natures and high frequency DNA can be damaged by exposure to toxic vaccines and drugs – many autistic children are damaged Indigos. They may also find it difficult to adapt to many mainstream activities or systems, such as the current, tightly controlled education system. Clearly seeing what is wrong with it, they will push against, or opt out of what is required of them. As a consequence many do not do well academically, although they are very bright and innovative.

The danger in all this is that Indigos might feel themselves isolated and not really aligned with the way things are on Planet Earth, and they may turn in on themselves in order to feel safe and as a way to cope in an uncaring world. Many Indigos find themselves taking drugs for mental health issues, depression and other psychological problems because they push against the mainstream and the dead weight of inertia here overwhelms them.

As a result they are likely to lose touch with who they are and their mission.

These are incredibly sensitive, high frequency souls and the density of Earth and the brutal systems in play here at the moment are very hard on them. Being born into an awake and aware family can give them a good head start, but without this many struggle.

It is also important that Indigos keep themselves grounded. There is much wrong here on Earth for a wide variety of reasons. Problems are easy to identify. Overthrowing these systems is part of what they are here to do, but they need to also have solutions waiting in the wings. It is not enough to be disruptive and destructive, they need to innovate and create and hold the Vision.

Star Family - Maldec

Maldec or Maldek as it is sometimes spelt, was a planet in our solar system, between Mars and Jupiter. At some point in the past it was destroyed. All that remains of it now is the rubble of the asteroid belt inhabiting its former orbit.

When this happened the explosion ripped the atmosphere from Mars and also pushed Earth from a stable 360 day orbit into an axial precessional wobble of 365 days.

It is also sometimes referred to as Tiamat, Phaeton or sometimes Elektra.

How was it destroyed? There are two main stories. The one which author and researcher Zecharia Zitchin gleaned from ancient Sumerian tablets he translated tells of a wandering planet called Nibiru, which enters our solar system every 3,600 years, and came too close to Maldec (which he calls Tiamat) and destroys it. Other similar versions tell of it being a comet, not a planet.

The other story is that there were three habitable planets in our solar system, Maldec, Mars and Earth. All had life on them. Both Mars and Maldec were more advanced than Earth. Either there was a war between the two, or a rouge comet which effectively destroyed both planets and caused devastation on Earth as giant chunks of rock rained down. Life survived here, but it was an extinction level event, and both humanity and animal and plant life had to rebuild from this.

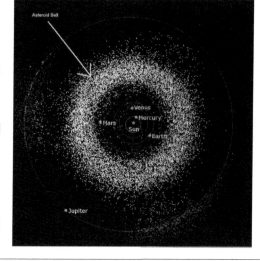

Which is true? I currently feel that whilst both have

something to offer, there is more to be understood, which my researches have yet to turn up. Obviously you have to make your own mind up.

The civilisation on Maldec was technologically advanced, although somewhat combative and warlike.

Souls of Maldecian origin are somewhat rare in coming into incarnation on the Earth, but those who do are very technologically minded, reflecting their planets focus. As you might expect from a technology driven, warlike society, they are also intelligent, have strong intellects, are analytical and good problem solvers. They are, however, usually not that emotionally well-developed and can struggle in developing their emotional intelligence.

They tend to be strong and focused in their beliefs, and it will take a lot of new information and time for them to digest and mull over this information before they might think of changing their mind.

When faced with choices they can over-think them. This is a result of karmic memory of the destruction of their planet and this echoes within them, leaving them fearful of the consequences of the choices they make, so they check and check again before committing to anything and can be very risk-adverse.

Whilst this can be annoying there is another aspect to this – this need to check thing thoroughly means they seek to see below the surface of what is going on, so they can often spot when things are wrong. They do not easily accept the surface explanation for something and are prepared to dig deeper to get at what is really going on.

This means they make excellent investigators or researchers of any sort.

Often reserved and self-contained they are careful whom they trust, but if you are accepted into their inner circle then they are loyal, loving and trustworthy friends, and they expect the same in return. They will only open up emotionally to those they completely trust.

For people who are very technologically orientated, Maldecians have a fascination with magic and the manipulation of energy. It is as if they suspect that technology is only part of the answer and they are missing something much deeper (which, of course, they are!). Tales of old, of mystery and imagination where magic abounds and heroes slay dragons and have honour and integrity at their heart find a resonance within them. King Arthur, Merlin, ancient gods and goddesses, the hero's journey will all be of interest to them.

Dysfunctional

The dysfunctional aspect of this Star Family can be a complete lack of emotional intelligence and an ensuing social awkwardness as a result. Rather than process emotions in a healthy way, they are likely to brood and fester and then blow up inappropriately when negative emotions are felt. This inevitably can lead to difficulty in relationships and a feeling of isolation as a result.

Another dysfunctional aspect can be where there is still a very strong sense of loss of their home planet, leading to feelings of not really belonging, wanting 'home' but unclear what they mean by this. It can leave them restless and unsettled as the trauma of the destruction of their home world is still felt within their subconscious. Taking steps to clear this trauma from their energy field can be of great help to these souls.

Star Family - Mars

When the planet Maldec exploded the surface atmosphere of Mars was almost completely stripped away, leaving only a very thin layer which was not conducive to life. Until this time a civilisation had flourished on Mars and abruptly came to a halt.

Their society was very patriarchal and hierarchical and was not very spiritual. Mars souls initially started incarnating on Earth, but it is rare for this to happen now, most of them choosing to go to other planets in the galaxy.

The sense of not belonging is one of the things which defines Mars souls incarnating on Earth. They tend to keep themselves to themselves and be quite reclusive, living quietly, not drawing attention to themselves. The current trend of over-sharing via social media is anathema to Mars souls and it is highly unlikely you will ever see them joining in!

As their society was highly structured and organised they are more comfortable incarnating into Far Eastern countries such as Japan, where there are far more rules and rigid social structure than in the West.

Where they do incarnate in the West is can be because at soul level they are trying to loosen up a little and be freer and more spontaneous, although much of Western life – indeed life on Earth – can seem too chaotic for them to be comfortable with it.

The military can be a natural fit for them – male-dominated, structured, rules-based and a channel for their

natural aggression. Mars was the God of War for a reason! Or they will be drawn to other structured, quiet environments where there may be a degree of anonymity. Within a University campus maybe, or the Civil Service or a large institution where the old-fashioned patriarchal ways still endure. The more structured the environment the better.

Although they tend not to feel very comfortable and are somewhat 'out of step' here, they are confident souls and tend not to suffer from self-doubt. They will not be found in the spotlight, but living quietly somewhere, not raising a rumpus – unless of course you poke the sleeping tiger. They have a warrior energy when roused and their natural aggression comes out.

It has been noticed that the few Mars souls who come to Earth tend to have a quite distinctive body shape or slightly-odd facial features in some way. They do not feel at home on this planet, and this can be reflected in their physicality. They can also have a very penetrating stare, whilst maintaining an impenetrable aura. This can make them seem a little secretive or mysterious.

Dysfunctional

The dysfunctional aspect of this Star Family can be their reclusiveness and their lack of engagement with society. Even if they are in a work environment they will be the employee who keeps themselves to themselves and does not join in, maybe working long hours and not seeking any real social life.

Because they are unlikely to engage much with colleagues, neighbours etc they can feel very lonely and isolated, which adds to their sense of being a stranger in a strange land.

Star Family - Mintaka

Mintaka is located within the constellation of Orion. Most of us are familiar with this constellation as it is one of the most recognisable in the night sky – particularly the three stars which make up Orion's belt.

Mintaka is the star at the right end of the three stars which make this up. Mintaka is a double-star system that once hosted a planet called Artuvia. Artuvia no longer is a habitable world.

Artuvia was a water world and the civilization there was unique in the galaxy in that it never made a choice which was away from the Light. It was 100% loyal to the Light and always aligned to this choice.

The Dark has always had a foothold in every other civilization which is part of the galactic family, but Mintaka had developed to the degree that no-one consciously made a negative choice - the choice was always in favour of the Light, to the extent that Mintakans see positive choices, choices for the Light as being the only choice to make.

Mintakans were the first group of soul families to ever incarnate on Earth in the wake of the Blueprinters who set things up here. It is estimated that this was as far back as 250,000 years ago, and they are one of the only Star Traveller groups to have been incarnating on Earth for nearly as long as the Blueprinters have.

But there is another reason as well – Mintaka is said to have acted as the original inspiration for the Earth Blueprint,

which is about the expression of Light in form and matter at a multidimensional level (we have a way to go to achieve this yet!)

The Mintakan civilization held – and Mintakan souls continue to hold – the pure vibration of Light. Mintakans do not acknowledge the Dark as a reality and demonstrate to the rest of the galaxy that it is not necessary to know Darkness in order to know Light.

Mintakans do not acknowledge this as a Truth – that in order to know Light you have to know Darkness - and for eons have demonstrated that the Light is not defined in any way by the Dark. It can shine powerfully and beautifully in its own right and does not need darkness to define it or bring it forth.

Light is all there is, it is the only choice, according to a Mintakan.

This means Mintakan souls have a difficult time understanding negativity and the wilful and purposeful negative choices made by many on this planet – to lie, to hurt others, to go to war…. They KNOW things can be much, much better, that it is possible to have a paradise here on Earth, which is such a beautiful and abundant planet. They KNOW that if we chose to create from Light and Light alone we could create this paradise easily and quickly.

Why wouldn't we choose that? Darkness brings fear and anger and shame and suffering whilst Light brings utopia. To a Mintakan there is no choice, and they are confused and unhappy as to why others can't see it.

Mintakans always see the Light, see the bright side. They create from Light and joy and happiness and are therefore much needed at this point in our planet's evolution. They hold within their soul the memory of creating from pure, unadulterated light, untainted by any darkness. Using this soul memory they can be a powerful force for good in the world.

Mintakans are often accused of having 'Pollyanna' tendencies. They are very open and trusting and are optimistic and see the positive potential clearly within others. Others around them can try to pull them down into their heavier, more complex, struggle-laden view of reality and some Mintakan souls, in order to fit in can dim their own Light. They don't want to be isolated, but need to be aware not everyone around them is willing to reach for the Light. Some like to stay stuck and stagnant in their dark, dank rut regardless. Rather than adapt to them Mintakans need to reach within and radiate as much pure light as they are capable of – and that is a lot!

Mintakans struggle to understand why anyone would make a choice that wasn't for the Light, it makes no sense to them. Others might try to take over or use their Light if they remain naïve at this level. They are not streetwise and need to get up to speed quickly about how power is used and abused on this planet. The Mintakan Light is not always welcomed by those who make choices out of fear or other negative patterns and they need to learn discernment and to assess accurately who is making a choice on the side of Light and who isn't.

They also need to avoid being pulled off course themselves by focusing on the fact that their Light comes from Source and can't be taken from them. If they focus on struggle and fear and negativity they will begin to lose this and find themselves adrift.

More than most Mintakans know that to hold the Light it is simply a matter of maintaining the right frequency – I say simply, but of course, here in deep matter, it is not so simple. But if anyone can do it, it is a Mintakan and they are great role models for the rest of us at this level. Do not fight Darkness, just radiate Light, joy, happiness etc. That is all that is needed to dispel Darkness.

So many fail to see that their 'war against Darkness' is approaching the issue at the wrong frequency. When we find Darkness in any form, we just need to breathe in Light, and lovingly expand it as much as we can for it to push back that Darkness. So simple.

One of the beautiful gifts Mintakans bring to Earth is that they see the best in others and can mirror it back to them. They see the potential within, that Divine spark of Light which can be grown, and are willing to invest in helping people do just that so they can fulfil that potential they see within.

They do need to be discerning about where they put their energy in this case though. By all means support and be the cheerleader for someone who is striving to be a better person, but do not waste time and energy of someone who chooses NOT to live up to their potential - and there are plenty who neither want nor are willing to make the effort to do this.

So one of their challenges is to learn to be discerning between what is potential and what is the reality of how a person is choosing to live – and this can usually be seen in the choices they are making. It is all very well to see the best in someone but only as long as that person is trying to live up to it not making choices which take them away from it! It is too easy for a Mintakan to take on people as 'projects' – this is particularly true of women in romantic relationships, so they need to beware picking a partner on the basis of what they could be, rather than what they are.

This needs to be applied to all areas of life. A business/romantic/other partner needs to be based on who this person is choosing to be, rather than the vision of what they could be. It is all too often a Mintakan will offer wholehearted support and help towards the vision of potential they see, whilst the other person just sits back and let them do all the heavy lifting!

Mintakans can be someone's greatest cheerleader, making excuses for unacceptable behaviour until such time as they eventually have to admit that, no matter how great the potential, it is not being lived up to. Thus, they are often left disappointed.

Mintakans are forgiving though – maybe too forgiving at times, giving second, third and fourth chances when most would have cut their losses.

They are however very optimistic and positive people, very loyal and trusting – their cup is half full, and they see every silver lining. They have an innate understanding of the difference between right and wrong and are natural uplifters and life enthusiasts, lovely to be around and curious. They are life-long learners – they find life a fascinating adventure and every day full of new discoveries.

When it comes to careers, any profession or job that is helping others to understand and see and grow the potential in themselves is ideal – they are excellent transformers! Coaching, self-development therapies, teaching or anything else that helps people see and develop their potential and shine their Light brighter is fulfilling for a Mintakan.

They also love variety and have a great need for it! They can have all sorts of hobbies and interests - a typical jack of all trades. It would not be unusual for a Mintakan soul to have lots of discarded hobbies around the house that they have tried before moving on.

This could lead to them 'shoulding' themselves whether it be at home or in the workplace – I should be more focused, I should stick with this even if it's not what I wanted/expected. We live in a society where pyramid building is exalted – working your way to excellence in one sphere. But Mintakans are more wall builders, and once they understand this is the way they approach life it can help them to see how variety is good for them. They are sampling all life has to offer and building up a broad range of experience and understanding.

Their growth and expansion lies in this variety. New things bring new understandings both of the world around them and insight into themselves. They integrate this and then move on to the next thing. The transformational value of whatever it is has been harvested so it is time to move on.

As a result they can make great entrepreneurs or small business owners where a wide variety of skills is a huge benefit, and they don't get bored easily.   If their work takes them into the corporate environment they need to ensure that there is plenty of variety and new experiences built into the job, otherwise they will get really bored quickly and days will drag.

Mintakans have a very real connection to water. Their home world, which is no longer inhabitable, was mainly made up of crystal clear water, so clear that you could see through it for miles, and they lived mainly in the water, although they did have the capability to walk on the land also. The water had a slightly different molecular structure to that here on Earth, so it was lighter, less dense.

Mintakans love being around water. It is a very healing element for them – living by or being near clear water is very rejuvenating. There is a dichotomy here though – as deep, dark water can be frightening to them. It is so unlike their soul memories. So although they are drawn to water, they don't like deep water. Often they don't necessarily have to go in water to feel the benefit, just being by it is soothing – even a bath can help them rebalance.

Many Mintakans have a vague longing for 'home' without knowing where home is – a soul memory for what has been lost. As a result they are great nesters, real home bodies, making a comfortable and safe environment for themselves. They also love working from home within the environment they have created.

Dysfunctional

Mintakans become dysfunctional when they overestimate someone's willingness to grow into their potential. The reality is that most people don't ever step up and into their potential, no matter how many chances they are given and how much help is offered – and Mintakans have a long pieces of elastic here, too long really! They will stick with trying to help someone realise their potential when in reality they need to learn to cut their losses.

As a result they can become very disillusioned and disappointed by others. Not only are they astonished by the poor choices and negativity people indulge in but they can start to feel their good nature is being taken advantage of by others. When this sense of disappointment and usage becomes frequent they can get very tired of planet Earth.

It can also lead to this Star Family becoming a control freak. They invest themselves heavily in people and can be so fixated on making the vision of what they see as someone's potential happen, they can try to make it happen FOR them.

People can become 'projects' that need fixing and they lose sight of free will.

This is the controlling mother or father or partner who refuses to let someone be who they chose to be, but tries to mould them to their own vision. Not only is this a waste of time, but worse still, they are ignoring their own potential and the fact they should be focusing on developing that rather than someone elses.

Star Family - Nihal

Nihal is the second brightest star in the constellation of Lepus, the Hare, and is sometimes called Beta Leporis, located below Orion's foot.

Nihalians are one of the "newer" Soul Groups on our planet. Although some Nihalian souls have had many incarnations here the majority do not have a long and consistent history of incarnating on Earth.

They only began arriving in significant numbers in the late '80s and '90s and some of the traits they brought with them were distinctive enough that they became referred to as the 'Indigo' and the 'Crystal' children, although, to be fair, the traits attributed to these are also shared in part at least by some other Star Families.

The Nihal Star Family as well as other star traveller groups (particularly Blueprinters, Mintakens and Pleidians) are coming here to aid in bringing about highly conscious vibrational change to our planet. They are Agents for Change and tend to arrive in a system only when big

change is imminent. At this level they are very selective in where and when they participate in a planet's evolution.

At this moment on Earth we are entering a period of not

just societal change, but also spiritual and technological. Energetically every aspect of life on Earth is being shaken up and Nihals are here to help in this process.

Nihalians are here to help show us a different way of doing things, they challenge the status quo, they question how things are done and are here to enable change at every level. They bring a modernising energy and are seeking through their work and their actions to progress society in a beneficial way.

Often working for non-profits, charities or organisations engaged with helping others they bring a modern and progressive energy to everything they do, a wonderful sense of freshness and youth with them, there is nothing stagnant about Nihalian energy!

Nihalians have strong self-esteem and value individuality. Despite this they are very aware of working and being part of a Collective.

Nihalians are very conscious and aware and have a naturally high level of intuition and most have at least one of the psychic senses – clairaudience, clairvoyance etc. As most are here on Earth for the first time they can be quite naïve around the way things are done on Earth. Some of these are simply Society's rules and rightly should be questioned, other aspects are to do with being here in physicality, something they are not used to and find quite hard. As a result many of those incarnating here for the first time have health challenges, particularly the first wave as they tried to adapt – but these often can be traced back to energetic imbalances and are usually best treated at this level rather than the physical.

There is a rebellious quality to Nihalian energy – all society's sacred cows and norms are to be questioned and challenged. Rather like children they are testing and stretching the rules to see if they are fit for purpose and serve the higher good of all. If not they are seeking to change them – something many still firmly entrenched in the old paradigm are finding very uncomfortable.

They can also generally see through the fears that adults try to hide. This can be confusing for them as children, as they try to make sense of what they see and 'know' versus what is being said.

Nihalians have been described as the quintessential millenials – creative and innovative thinkers, looking for better ways of doing things, using their rebellious streak to force change, aware of the power of technology and social media and able to think outside the box. They also work well at the Collective level, coming together in groups to achieve things.

Technology holds no fears for them and any kind of virtual connection, such as social media, they understand how to use to its full effect. Nihalians notice what others see and value and share this through various media so can spread an idea or concept very quickly. They can be Way Showers for helping guide mass consciousness.

They can find it hard to work within the corporate world as they do not take to authority well – they will not bow to authority just because it is the way in this Society. They question and will respect if respect is due based on actions and achievements not position or status. They will probably be more comfortable being their own boss and showing us all new and unconventional ways of working that bring better work-life balance.

Nihals are here to help us question the existing structures and systems and to help create a fairer world that works for all. Old, outdated systems have to go and they are part of the redefining that is happening all around us, but care needs to be taken not to throw the baby out with the bath water, and what is good and functional is not trashed alongside what isn't working just for the sake of it.

Deeply committed to the betterment of this world Nihalians consider they are here to
- do good in this world
- learn all they can about living here
- make a difference

- make friends
- help people
- have fun

The have fun bit is very important. This should not be hard work! There should be plenty of play and laughter and they are here to remind us of this. For a long time we have forgotten this aspect of experiencing life in physicality and it is past time to be reminded of it.

Dysfunctional

The dysfunctional aspect of this Star Family is entitlement. Here on Earth every action has a consequence and what you want has to be balanced alongside responsibilities and 3D reality.

Wanting and expecting to have the latest shiny iPhone is all very well, but here in current 3D reality it is not just a question of saying 'Make it so!' It has to be bought with real money which comes from parents, or a job or suchlike. These are the hard realities of 3D living here on Earth.

Wanting all the bright shiny toys, opportunities to travel and having fun etc that Society can offer is all very well, but none of it comes free and under current circumstances it has to be earnt. Expecting otherwise is entitlement. I feel like such a party pooper saying this, but unfortunately it is our current stark reality.

We live within a consensual reality here and the understanding of what that is may need to be changed to something more inclusive, equal and fairer, but there is no magic wand to be waved to make it happen. It takes vision and work – and Nihalians are here to help with this!

Question and rebel by all means but real change takes effort and needs substance to it. Some young Nihalians feel it is enough to rebel and state an intention and that will get great results, overlooking the fact it takes hard graft to come up with new rules and structures to replace those which are crumbling, and that these are needed to give the framework for

Society to operate in – not to mention the shifting of consensus realities at the energetic level that are needed in order for critical mass to be reached.

Visions of Utopia need to be grounded in practicality and functionality, and rebelling against one set of rules is fine, but they are only going to be replaced by another set (hopefully better!) so you'd better work out what they need to be.

To bring real results any rebellion needs to have worked out what it is seeking to put in place otherwise it can leave a vacuum into which undesirable outcomes can slip.

Break existing rules by all means, but do so responsibly and with a clear intention of what you want to replace them with – new rules and structures that give real results. And then do what it takes to make it happen. Nihalians can do this but not if they get stuck in the 'I just want to have fun/be famous/do what I want' rut whilst expecting others to provide the means to do this.

Yes, it sucks. But if you don't like it, change it. Put in the foundations for a totally different way for *everyone* to live in a more equal, fun, inclusive way. You know <u>how</u> deep in your cell tissue, you really do!

Taken to the extreme a Nihalian can withdraw from a Society they don't really like the look of and create their own 'virtual world' using the technology around them. Retreating into their own world may be one way of coping, but it does nothing to help the Collective or be the Change Bringers Nihalians are here to be.

See also: Indigo Races, as most Nihalians fit this template.

Star Family - Ophiuchus

Ophiuchus is a constellation which straddles the celestial equator and is often called the Serpent Bearer and is represent as a man grasping, or wrestling with a serpent. It is said to depict the Greek god, Apollo, wrestling with the great Python of the oracle at Delphi for control of this temple.

It is also sometimes referred to as the 13th Zodiac sign. Little is known about Ophiuchan Starseeds as they are so rare. Few chose to incarnate here on Earth, although it is said that some of the various Ophiuchan races did visit here during very early Egyptian times.

They have energetic forms, although they can take on something more physical for periods of time, and are a race of noble character, high integrity and values, and gentle, loving and kind. They also have telepathic abilities and find the levels of dishonesty, deception, unkindness and bullying endemic on Earth hard to bear.

The few Starseeds who do incarnate here can seem to be 'push-overs' due to their gentle nature and lack of 'street smarts', but when someone crosses a line they find out just how strong minded and strong-willed they really are, and how high their moral code is.

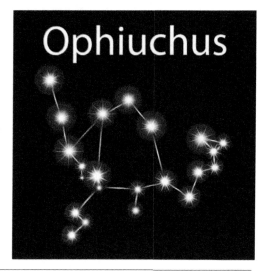

They are likely to be reclusive, and are life's observers and have an inbuilt radar honed for bullshit and those who are not being 'real' with them. Ophiuchans are loving and wise in a way rarely seen on Earth.

Star Family - Parallels

Parallels are not from a star or galaxy within the reality that we are aware of. They are literally from one of the Parallel realms which exist alongside ours and live in a Parallel multidimensionality alongside ours.

Furthermore, they also have the experience to exist in more than one parallel universe and live and experience them at the same time.

Scientists talk of the possibility of there being other realities that exist alongside our universe, separated by a thin veil between – Parallels have soul aspects on both sides of these veils, their consciousness being anchored in two or more parallel universes.

Why might they do this? We have a set of Universal Laws here which define, at the energetic level, how our universe works. Are these the same across all parallel universes? Probably not. So one of the reasons Parallels might want to come here is to experience some aspects of our universe that don't exist in theirs – gender maybe, or physicality or the laws of polarity.

Another reason might be for spiritual advancement or to experience the human emotional body (which is not universal). Or maybe they are just explorers and travellers so they are here just because they can be – much like we go on holiday somewhere for the experience of a different culture and landscape.

So while Parallels might feel slightly out of place, or feel like they are on the outside of a culture they are also here to enjoy

themselves, and pick up a variety of experiences and sample much of what Earth has to offer.

Unlike most of the star traveller groups which come to Earth they are not here helping – or hindering – with Earth and humanity's evolution. That is not their purpose, although they can and do participate where they feel inclined. Rather they are here for themselves, although that does not mean they have nothing at all to contribute to helping humanity advance. Many choose to take on roles which actively help us expand our understanding of what is possible.

As they are not fully anchored here they can often seem not fully grounded or engaged with things on this plane, and not fully present in their own lives. Some can seem to lack ambition or not really have goals other than drifting through trying this and that. Often they will do their best to fit in, adopting social conventions and seeking conformity in the effort to pass as 'one of us'. For the sharp-eyed and discerning however there is an 'otherness' about them, and they can almost seem to be shape shifters at times as they morph to fit in with different groups.

Within them they hold the key to an opening energetic portal of interdimensional travel between their universe and ours or maybe more even! The thought of having aspects of ourselves living lives elsewhere can seem confusing to most Earthers as things are very linear here, but Parallels have no effort in understanding this concept. They usually have an awareness of being 'somewhere else' for at least part of their time, as they focus more of their attention on another aspect of themselves elsewhere. Their awareness is not fully here. Daydreaming is not unusual or a sense of floating and detachment but despite this there is not a wavering sense of Self. On the contrary they have a very strong sense of Self, just one that is spread over different dimensions.

Unlike many other Star Families who incarnate here and don't feel 'at home' or experience feelings of limitation or restriction, Parallels rarely feel this. They know life is expansive, that the possibilities of self-expression over multiple universes and timelines exists and can be enjoyed. Their understanding of themselves as not just as a universal, galactic being but as a multidimensional one as well can really help us here on Earth, with our more limited understanding of who we are, as we begin to take the blinkers off at this time of evolution and change.

It goes without saying that Parallels have much they can teach us if we care to be open to it. They have knowledge of other dimensions and ways of being and knowledge held within them they can access if appropriate. Often our problem here is that if they tend to begin to speak of this we just consider them weird as it is so far outside our experience.

Star Family - Pleiades

The Pleiades is a cluster of stars in the constellation of Taurus often called The Seven Sisters. In Greek mythology these were the daughters of the Titan Atlas and sea nymph Pleione.

Pleiadians are one of the groups which has been connected to Earth and her evolution for a very long period of. So they are deeply linked to the seeding of consciousness not just on this planet but on others in the cosmos, and provide help to these planets and populations not just through coming into incarnation to help influence things, but also through 'off world' help and guidance channelled through some human individuals (although beware imposter beings masquerading as helpful Pleiadians!).

One of the most defining aspects of Pleiadians is that they are Agents for Change. They are catalysts for rapid change, and can be like a breath of fresh air blowing through – or a hurricane wreaking havoc, depending on your perspective on change of course!

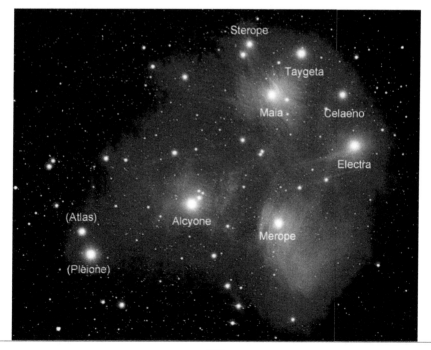

As individuals they are energetic, dynamic, inspirational and are also excellent communicators. They can hold and communicate a vision that will inspire you to take action. They are excellent motivational speakers and writers as a result, although it has to be said that they are not very good on the detail. Pleiadians tend to find this aspect both boring and frustrating and want to get to their goal....NOW! So to harness their inspirational and visionary abilities a Pleiadian needs to learn to delegate to someone, or have a team in place, who will implement the step-by-step process that gains the goal and handles all the necessary planning and detail. Pleiadians are starters, so they need to team with finishers.

Pleiadians are unafraid of change and like to get on with it – they are not people who tend to take a long time thinking about changing something, or getting used to what it might feel like or mean, they just get on with it. Their motto is JUST DO IT!

They can sometimes invoke the law of unintended consequences by trying to move too quickly and not thinking through long term consequences. Usually by the time these manifest a Pleiadian has moved on to the next project and someone else is left mopping up behind them. Being fast-paced isn't always beneficial, especially when some necessary steps are skipped to speed things up. Again, ideally a Pleiadian needs to be partnered with someone who can offset this tendency and is a natural foil for their quicksilver ideas and energy.

Pleiadian souls need to slow down on occasion and take a hard look at themselves. Because they tend to move fast and rarely think through the consequences many Pleiadian souls unintentionally fall into negative ways of being or end up on less than positive career paths. It is estimated that incarnated Pleiadians are roughly divided half and half between negative and positive souls. This is not because they set their intent this way, but because they don't take the necessary time to set clear intentions and check out consequences or think things fully through before they charge ahead. The road to hell, as they say, is paved with good intentions.

As I have said they are very active visionaries and very powerful communicators and very inspiring orators. And this can be a double-edged sword. They can inspire others with their big vision and bring them with them, creating great vistas which open people up to new possibilities and potentials, so they had better ensure that they are heading in the right direction!

This makes them potentially great leaders, but they MUST have the backup necessary to implement. They are big picture people rather than fine detail. And at times of big shift and change they are just what we need to stir things up. But they can skip the planning or fail to put in place the necessary steps as they want to achieve their vision fast, and it can fail at this point.

They also make great teachers, as they can inspire but again, need to focus on the abilities of who they are teaching not rush ahead and lose them in their enthusiasm.

They are also highly verbal and can excel in marketing, PR and sales as well as being great storytellers. Properly harnessed to a function which brings benefit to all their gifts can be extraordinary, but in harness to corporate greed and consumerism they won't necessarily bring positive benefit to the Collective however. There is a saying 'Just because you can, doesn't mean to say you should', and Pleiadians maybe need to question 'Is this for the highest good of all' before they hare off after another goal.

This can be important to note for a Pleiadian because they carry a very heart-based, loving and sensitive energy and are often high functioning empaths. This means they need to be very careful to make positive choices because if their choices orient them with more negative forces it can impact their health and well-being very quickly.

Charismatic and charming Pleiadians love to be the centre of attention, and left unchecked this can become quite prima-donna-like. Ego needs to be in service to the heart. They love an audience – the bigger the better. They are not backward in expressing their opinions and thoughts, but just need to be aware that it is not always appropriate, and not everyone wants to be on the end of their unsolicited advice, no matter how well-meaning.

Again, it all comes back to slowing down a little and taking time to think things through.

With their dynamic energy Pleiadians have a strong relationship with sex and sensuality, and if they choose to explore sacred sex as an expression of unconditional love and connection it can become a very powerful tool for energetic work.

Most Pleiadians have a love of technology, and indeed some Pleiadians souls incarnating here are helping to inspire the development of earth-based communications and technology – internet, mass media, television, telecommunications all appeal to them as a means of reaching larger audiences.

They also have a radar for the next exciting trend which can serve them well in this field. They make good entrepreneurs as well as excelling in product innovation and development.

It is not unusual to find a Pleiadian at the centre of a revolution – they are the change bringers and nothing does this faster than a revolution! And yet so many revolutions fail due to poor planning and implementation. Enthusiasm and conviction are not enough.

There are strong healer qualities on many levels in many Pleiadians. Being empathic if they develop their ability to catalyse energy and help others move out of stuckness and victimhood they can move individuals forward quickly.

Overall, Pleidians have a great deal to offer us here on Earth at this time, helping inspire us with expanded goals and dreams and to move forward quickly, not procrastinate and dither, provided they have good self-awareness of some of the pitfalls.

Dysfunctional

It can be quite easy for the many Pleiadian talents to become negatively expressed and dysfunctional.

In their desire to get somewhere fast they can skip vital steps, and go for the quick fix which sabotages what they want to achieve. They can take shortcuts which are not necessarily above board and can also begin to see people as a resource to be used to achieve a goal, and with their charming inspirational and communication abilities they can start to become manipulative and use others as stepping stones leaving people feeling used and taken in as things come crashing down.

A Pleiadian making poor choices can spin a good story and have no issues around elaborating on the truth, so they can become very good fraudsters and con artists. They are also very good at justifying to both themselves and others how they achieve their ends – the ends justifies the means could be another motto! Of course, it doesn't, but they have the gift of the blarney stone and can delude themselves as well as others.

They also need to beware coming up with highly impractical visions. They build great castles in the air which sound wonderful but have no foundation.

A negative Pleiadian soul can also execute what is called a 'karmic dump' where they have found a way to get round karmic law by convincing other souls to take over their karma for completion here on Planet Earth, leaving them with what is called negative unjustified karma.

This is not to take away from all the wonderful things Pleiadians can accomplish here on Planet Earth – it is just necessary to check out their orientation first!

Star Family - Polaris

Polarians come from the star system of Polaris, the North or Pole Star, a beacon of light for travellers for millennia.

The North Star has served as a dependable and consistent point of focus to help guide and direct humanity through the unknown since history began.

And this sums up Polarians. They embody the qualities of true north - loyalty, constancy and consistency. They can be counted on – they are dependable, 'the rock', being very practical and down-to-earth.

They also have an instinctive understanding of the universal axiom 'All is One'. Deeply sensed within them, they are a unifying force, they bring this sense of wholeness with them which is magnetic to those deeply entrenched in separation consciousness. This vibration of wholeness can help to remind others that beyond the illusion of separation everything in the Universe comes from a single Source. We are ultimately all unified in that Light and consciousness.

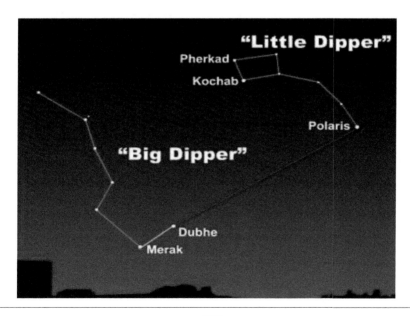

There is a deep Truth regarding the Blueprint we come from – it has been designed on the basis of unity in diversity. We all come from the one wholeness, the one Source, no matter what shape, size, colour, makeup or type of being we might be.

Whilst the endless diversity we see here on Planet Earth embodies just some of the many ways that universal consciousness can create and express itself, it still springs from the same Source. And Polarians are here on Earth to remind us, help us back to the remembrance of this Truth: Unity in diversity.

And they are here to help us move towards a way of living on this planet which is honouring of this principle. They celebrate diversity and what unifies us, and have much to teach us at this time.

It is one of the distortions of the Earth Blueprint which is having to be addressed. Whilst polarity and separation are part of being here on Planet Earth it was not meant to play out in quite the way it has. True polarity is that of opposites – up and down, dark and light, positive and negative, hot and cold. Within this polarity there is immense opportunity for diversity – and yet it also has an inherent stability to it. At the same time separation was not meant to be seen and experienced in the form of separation from Light, but rather as the opportunity for individuation, for an expression of uniqueness whilst being part of the whole.

This seeming dichotomy is something Polarians absolutely understand and hold the balance point of this understanding within them – that we are all different, all unique, but that we are also One. They bring this consciousness to Earth and help 'tune' others back into this vibration and therefore adjust the field of Collective Consciousness of Earth in this respect.

It can be hard on Polarians, raised within the 3D matrix of Earth to remember this – the forces of separation and division are strong, particularly at the moment. But as soon as they tune back into this Truth within them, and stay true to this – their own North Star – they help to bring others into this frequency.

This energy of oneness ensures that Polarians are the 'glue' that holds any group together be it family, organisations, teams etc. They have a way of gathering and keeping people together for a common cause. This is not natural leadership but has its place.

They know the whole is greater than the sum of its parts, and unity is the Polarian ideal but they need to remember that this needs to be balanced with individualism.

As you might expect for beings who hold this Truth, they are not fans of the hierarchical systems of Earth. The type of hierarchy we see around us, which brings an imbalance of power, privilege, wealth, opportunity etc is a dysfunctional distortion of the working of polarity.

Polarians automatically reject this – they see all beings as equal. They manage by consensus – it is the principle of the Round Table which makes sense to them, where all are equal and all have equal input. Current hierarchies are anathema to them and when they have to participate in this system they will either seek to change it or go elsewhere as its inherent unfairness is something they cannot live with long term.

All are equal, there is no judgment of difference and they can bring in that balance point to any group, which is so beautifully expressed by the yin/yang symbol of the East.

They are great team members and team builders, and bring people together and can be great assets to any organisation at this level. They are very inclusive and love to engage others in mutual decision-making processes. They need to remember that not everyone wants this, and many need room to breathe. It can be a critical learning experience for a Polarian to let everyone make their own decisions and trust them to do so.

Within partnership, be it marriage or business, they love making decisions together, working in a way that is inclusive.

Utterly reliable and trustworthy Polarians can be loyal to a fault and stay in situations long after they cease to serve them. They need to learn to be loyal to themselves and their needs first and others second rather than stick with something to the bitter end which is not serving them. Teaching a Polarian this from a young age can be a great gift. Loyalty is a gift to Self, and is not about misplaced loyalty to those who, very often, do not deserve it.

Once they do this there is an innate integrity which ensures that they make congruent choices.

Unusually, Polarian have two points of vibration – a high point and a low point. They work mainly from the low point of vibration, which helps to keep them grounded, and live and work in a steady, predictable way.

It is from the high point of their vibration that they receive intuition and communicate with the Spirit world. This is simple for them to tune into during meditation or – once they are aware of it – by simply shifting their point of focus to this higher vibration at any moment.

They tend to be very slow in making decisions and life changes – they consider it from all angles and take time, maybe years, thinking it through, but once their mind is made up nothing stands in their way. They find change hard, so tend to want to make big changes all at once, rather than incrementally. So they need to really think out any big moves and work out the big leap, not little steps – this is true whether they are making life changes or within the work environment.

However, when they chose to work from their higher point of vibration things can happen very quickly and they can speedily move towards goals. They often engage this after having taken time to think things through!

Many may see a Polarian make a HUGE life change and think it is sudden and rash, little realising they have taken years to make their minds up and plan our what is needed.

They are steady and comfortable presences and very family-oriented, as well as being intensely loyal. They can also be quite single-minded to the point of stubbornness, trustworthy and make excellent partners and friends because of their dependability and reliability.

A Polarian who has managed to overcome or not take on too much societal conditioning can truly begin to demonstrate to others how to integrate mind, body and spirit. As part of the human experience is sensing the gaps within – whether it be health, relationships, personality, purpose etc - and working out how to fill them a Polarian can be an excellent role model in this respect.

They are sensitive to the changing pole shift currently (Polaris is moving away from true north due to the Precession of the Equinoxes) and this can also lead to them feeling unsettled and becoming stuck to compensate.

Polarians also have a tendency to be affected by earth energies and seismic movements – earthquakes, volcanoes etc. – makes them unsettled and can upset their equilibrium for days. Energy lines and changing magnetics also affect them – so they need to be aware of this and check out where they live for any problems.

The changing vibrationary rate of the Earth, and all on her, is also something they will be sensitive to, but awareness of this, and their ability to be very grounded in the way they live can help us all navigate the changes which are under way.

Dysfunctional

As usual there can be a dysfunctional aspect to this group – they can become very stuck and stagnant whether it be in a situation, thinking, habits, attitudes etc. At its worst they can insist on following a path through thick and thin which clearly does not serve them and refuse to re-consider the choices they are making.

This stubbornness can become a block to diversity, and become a single-minded tenacity to the path they are following to the detriment of the many other paths to wholeness.

They need to remember 'Diversity in Unity' and pin this up where they will see it daily!

They can also become stuck and stagnant if they come to a point where they begin to see change – and rapid change is underway all around us – as something that will take them away from the all-important sense of wholeness. They need to remember that wholeness is dynamic, constantly renewing its expression of itself and is a living thing that needs to be explored, its many avenues followed.

Unity in Diversity, always they need to come back to this.

This sense of stagnation can also come in as part of a sense of overwhelm when they look at the chaos and confusion in the world right now and want to withdraw and shut down in response.

Polarians also need to understand that a lack of self-awareness can lead to them investing in an incongruent self-image – and getting stuck in it despite its obvious shortcomings and lack of authenticity. Being true to what is truly important to them – not a societal imposed construct – and being authentic in the expression of this is the answer.

Star Family - Procyon

Procyon is the brightest star in the constellation of Canis Minor, a binary star system, and the eighth brightest star in the night sky. It is also sometimes referred to as the Little Dog Star.

We don't know a huge amount about Procyonians as they are quite a rare Starseed group. This is because many ages ago Procyon put an energetic shielding around their planet, at the time of the Draconian takeover of Hadar.

For many years they had suffered continual raids from one of the Anunnaki races who coveted their genetics, stealing them to produce an attractive-looking, human seeming race whose home is in the Pleiades, and who are one of the aggressive intruder races causing havoc here on Earth, named the Nordics, due to their pretty features and blond hair and blue eyes from the genetics stolen from the Procyonians.

With continual Anunnaki raids, and then the Dracos looking to become a threat they decided to cut themselves off in order to be safe, by erecting an impenetrable shield.

That shielding has kept any Procyonian souls who were away at the time travelling other systems unable to get home. They were simply shut out at the time the barrier went up and so they incarnate on places like Earth as their home system is barred to them – although it is said that recently this interdiction is about to be or has been lifted.

This may mean we will see more Procyonians in future.

So Procyonian souls are often a little lost and can seem quite aimless with no clear 'mission' here on Earth - although this is not all the Truth. There are some Procyonian souls here who chose to be here and contribute to the coming Shift and as a result are much more focused and purposeful.

Those who fall into this latter group will be hard working – sometimes to the point of being workaholic – and are drawn to technology and how things work and can be improved to change the world around us – the way we produce food, or energy for example – and find visualising complex and abstract ideas and concepts easy.

They are also likely to be analytical, are tenacious in achieving a goal, and do not change their minds easily once they have made it up. They also have a strong sense of helping others, working for the improvement of all wherever possible and are great problem solvers.

There would seem to be a body type for the Procyonians who are here – they are usually of slight build, with a slim to thin body and often unusual mesmerising eyes. They usually have the pretty features, blond hair and blue eyes the Anunnaki so desired. They don't need huge amounts of food to keep them going and are usually into healthy eating. It is said that some Procyonians practice breatharianism.

It is not unusual for a Procyonian to feel quite isolated – there are not many of them here after all, and it is unlikely they will meet another Procyonian.

All Procyonians are drawn to sunshine. In order to flourish they need to be outdoors and in the sun and light. They have the quirk of using the Sun's rays as a source of nourishment and energy. This is not done consciously but they assimilate solar energy and can use it for their benefit. Indeed, they need it for wellbeing, it is a necessity for them, and therefore naturally they seek sunshine and warmth.

They will generally have a skin which tans well and easily. They also generally enjoy the physicality of being in a body and tend to look after it well, exercising and eating healthily. They also enjoy loving relationships.

Many Procyonians have psychic gifts, specifically at the kinaesthetic/empathic level. Indeed, they tend to work through the physical body in all they do, and have more sense than most of the energetic aspect that underpins our physicality. They therefore understand energy healing modalities and can be natural energy workers, and have an innate understanding that many other Starseeds have barely begun to get to grips with.

The process of Ascension, be it planet or human, is about raising frequencies and tapping into higher energies and timelines. Procyonians can help us understand that whilst meditation is one route, the physical body and its potential is another – very effective - route to spiritual development.

We live in the shadow of world religions that for many centuries have taught that the physical body is sinful and bad, more often to be punished than praised or enjoyed. Procyonians know better and enjoy every aspect of the amazing vehicle within which their consciousness resides, and can help us shed the millennia of conditioning we have around this.

Procyonians who have washed up on the shores of Planet Earth because they have nowhere else to go often don't have a clear connection to a sense of purpose for incarnating here, as I have said. One of the ways they can make the best of the situation they are in is to find someone who *does* have a clear sense of purpose and take up a support role with them. By becoming part of the team enabling someone with a clear vision or mission to 'deliver' this, they in turn give meaning to their incarnation here.

This is not the same as being a follower in the train of a guru for example, or part of someone's congregation, or buying into any crackpot philosophy. Discernment is needed so that their considerable resources are being channelled into supporting something and someone that really does have the potential to change the world for the better.

Those Procyonians who are here with a sense of mission, having chosen to be here will, at some level, be tuned into being a Warrior for the Light in some way. Their own home planet is forbidden to them as it has been trying to protect itself from takeover by Dark Forces and they are prepared to fight and help this Planet to resist and find ways to free Earth from the negative influences of other less than benign races which cause disruption and bring Darkness to Earth and humanity.

They can do this simply by tapping into the core of who they are – beings of Light, who take pleasure and joy in their physical bodies bringing joy to the simple things in life which are accessible to all – the feel of sunlight on the skin, the beauty of nature, the pleasures inherent in our senses when we stop and tune into them fully, as well as using their considerable gifts around being able to imagine new, better timelines and technologies to improve things here on Earth.

Dysfunctional

The dysfunctional aspect of this soul family inevitably relates to the aimless quality they can have. If they do not address this they can end up drifting and contributing or achieving nothing of any value – and certainly nothing that satisfies their desire to see change for the better.

It can be a fine line between supporting someone in a common goal or vision and becoming dependent or passive in handing over the responsibility to someone else to give their life meaning and purpose.

This can lead to very dysfunctional relationships as well as working environments, where the attachment becomes obsessive and unhealthy. There should always be equal value exchange which takes place, no matter the scenario - romantic relationship, work relationship etc.

Anything else can lead a Procyonian who feels aimless to hitch their wagon to someone elses star out of a kind of desperation to give meaning to their existence rather than from a place of deep conviction that this is the right thing to do.

Star Family - Sirius

Sirius is a star in the constellation Canis Major, and is also called the Dog Star. It is the brightest star in the night sky and is a binary system around 20 times brighter than our sun.

There is a rich folklore that links Sirius to ancient civilisations. The Dogon tribe in Africa have a tradition of contact with beings from Sirius and astronomical knowledge about the Sirius system which has only recently been verified – so how have they held this knowledge for thousands of years?

There is a strong link with the Ancient Egyptians, who aligned their temples to this star. The heliacal rising of Sirius (when it becomes visible again after a period of been hidden by daylight) marked the start of the yearly Nile inundation which was so central to Egypt's fertility. It was also personified in the form of the goddess Sopdet, as well as having strong links to Isis and Osiris.

Symbolically Sirius is said to embody the principle to guide, protect and lead those who seek Light, and as it burns brightly it represents the highest aspiration to Truth and to being the best we can be.

So Sirians have been incarnating on the Earth for millennia, and are very linked to Earth and her Blueprint. They are noble and high-ranking ambassadors of the Guardian Alliance[9], and

Sirius

Canis Major

---

[9] See Appendix C

197

are known on Earth for honouring what serves humanity best, having a high level of integrity. They have a reputation for helping to uncover and bring out the best that any world has to offer and will fight to bring souls back to Truth.

Sirians tend to be found incarnating on Earth when there is the potential for advancement to existing civilisations – many were to be found here during not just the Ancient Egyptian, but the Atlantean civilisation before that. Whenever there is the potential for significant advancement and change, both technologically and spiritually, they will arrive.

This is partly because Sirians honour all that is true, and are warriors for justice and balance and seek to achieve the highest potential of what is possible, partly because they love improving things.

There is also the fact that Sirians do also have a sense of responsibility around much of the warfare which has taken place on Earth. Sirians love technology and have a highly advanced technological civilisation, and the spiritual maturity to go with it. They wish to share all they have and know with others, to offer improvements to other civilisations, and have done so in the past with civilisations here on Earth, without fully realising that most Earthers do not have a sufficient level of maturity to handle advanced technology for the higher good of all – particularly when there are fallen races manipulating their consciousness in a destructive way. They also did not bear in mind that these forces on the Earth with negative intentions of control and power could, and did, gain control of and subvert the gifts into weaponry which caused massive destruction.

Atlantis is a case in point. An advanced civilisation which used crystal technology much of which was gifted by the Sirians, it destroyed itself through misuse of this technology[10].

---

[10] In truth the Atlantean cataclysm was largely caused by the Atlanteans being led astray and manipulated by the negative Sirian-Anunnaki Fallen Race, amongst others, as distinct to the Sirians of the Emerald Covenant.

At a subconscious level there can be a Collective awareness of their part in these catastrophes of the past, and as a consequence if this has not been addressed and released a Sirian soul who has incarnated on Earth to help improve things can feel a sense of fear and caution around fully stepping into their power here, and stepping forwards as they have a subconscious concern around the consequences of their actions.

This hampers them in their mission as they have much help to offer at this time. Fortunately most Sirians incarnating here have addressed the issue of over eagerness to share their technological knowledge and learned to be more discerning in how and when they do so.

Sirians are warriors for justice and balance and will fight to help each Soul Family in the universe reach its full potential for the expression of its unique gifts and Blueprint. They, along with other Starseed Families are here on Earth at this time to help re-align with her original Blueprint.

Sirians have a great gift for improving things! If they had a motto, it would be "Let's find a better way!" And this relates to every aspect of life, not just machine-based technology.

Their creativity is inspired by existing structures and systems. They are not inventors – they did not invent the wheel - they just made the wheel rounder, faster, and more efficient with their creativity and innovative thinking. So they are masters of improving what already exists, or combine and re-assemble what already exists in a new way. They tend not to be innovators, but improvers.

This is something Sirian souls really need to recognise in themselves - that their gift is to figure out how to improve what is already there. But they need a productive outlet for their need to implement improvements in existing structures and systems. The intellectual property or copyright often belongs to someone else, so Sirians can tend to copy or plagiarize (especially if they are fifth energy centre) and if they are not aware of this tendency they can end up simply tweaking existing modalities which are not theirs, rather than re-inventing them in a creative, distinctive and improved way.

This can frustrate them if they are looking to be innovative, which is not their strength. However, they can innovate through improving existing models, technologies and systems and can be highly creative and original in this way.

Sirians are always looking for how things can be improved by moving it to a higher expression of itself or a better way of working. This is intrinsic to their nature and relates to structures, people, organisations, social constructs etc.

Sirians love structure and organisation. They are even very comfortable within hierarchy, so work well within organisations. They are drawn to hold integrity in all they do and within organisations can keep the vision of the higher road alive to ensure its delivery. They do not do well in corrupt and greedy organisations though and soon learn to contribute their gifts to those more aligned to the higher good.

They bring not just integrity to what they do but also a sense of organisation and logic, of method and process and planning. They love systems, lists, methodologies, calendars, mind map systems, spreadsheets. Within an organisation they can improve a system to become more efficient if they are trusted to do so.

Even Sirians who are entrepreneurs like to have things clearly defined and structured. They make fantastic business consultants where they have well defined roles of accountability, delegation etc. and can help improve such things as efficiency and productivity within any organisation they are let loose within! They also do well in fields such as accountancy, project management and finance – in fact anything which requires structure, organisation and clear methodology laid out.

The one proviso here is that the corporate goal of self-serving and greed may leave them feeling out of alignment with serving the greater good, so they may seek to shift to an expression of their career that allows a more aligned way of working. Or maybe they can bring change to the culture of a company from the inside? Who knows? With a Sirian, anything is possible.

They can do particularly well as turnaround specialists, helping to rescue something that is failing and setting it back on its feet before moving onto the next project.

Their love of improvement extends to self-improvement as well as helping others develop and evolve, so they can often become involved in the world of personal development and transformation.

They are also always looking for 'the better way' – whether that is someone's spiritual path, their approach to life, improving a company or even a country. They help to show how new technologies can be used for a higher purpose than war and destruction.

Those with Sirius as their system of origin are very focused, very determined and set on whatever path they decide. A Sirian soul does not change its mind easily, they hold to their own Truth very strongly, but if they can be convinced that a new "path" is more appropriate, they will put the same kind of focus on the new, and release the old quickly. Sirians have strong beliefs, ideals and personal integrity.

They make very trustworthy and loyal friends and can be very hurt and disillusioned if others whom they invite into their inner circle do not act likewise. It is an honour to be the close personal friend of a Sirian soul.

A hallmark of the Sirian soul can be that they are considered dreamers, or be considered forgetful or unobservant as they are simply elsewhere. They have a vivid, active inner life, whilst presenting a calm and reserved outer appearance. Indeed this trait in Sirian children can lead to them being 'diagnosed' with learning or attention disorders, when it is simply that they are disinterested in the way they are being taught.

Sirians dislike war, understanding the futility of it. Even war movies are not entertaining to them. They will therefore work tirelessly with organisations trying to broker and maintain peace and help a country build its strengths and work with others in harmony, not attack them. This is one of the great gifts they are bringing to our war-torn planet, wanting to lift us out of this dynamic and into a place of peaceful co-existence.

It is not that Sirians can't fight – they have been part of many wars throughout the universe to uphold Divine Truth and Justice, always on the side of Light. They have seen how futile war is, and how damaging to all involved, and that there are really no winners. You are more likely to find them as part of the Peace Corps than the regular army.

Another Sirian aspect is the ability to balance both the male and female aspect within. Their energy at this level is very balanced and projects a sense of wholeness. Whatever their sex, they can express either male or female energies easily and are not hung up on gender specific roles. They have no desire for the archetypal 'battle of the sexes' within a relationship and this lack of competition within a relationship can be very refreshing as they seek to co-create within the union, not compete.

When functioning well Sirians are a role model for others as to how men and women can work in partnership, co-creating together from a point of wholeness not co-dependency. As such they can be valuable role models, working with the Collective to bring balance in this way.

Dysfunctional

The major dysfunctional aspect of Sirians can be a lack of originality. As already discussed they are great at taking existing structures and modalities and being very inventive in the way they can change them for the better.

As has already been stated, merely tweaking something though is encroaching on someone else's intellectual property and can see them courting trouble. The improvement needs to be substantial and creative before they start claiming it as their own. Ripping someone off may not be their intent, but can be the consequence when they do not fully embrace the major changes and innovations they are capable of doing.

Another expression of this can be when they aggressively embrace religious or corporate values or someone's teachings and seek to become 'the best' at what they have adopted. This can lead to very rigid behaviour in policing and upholding the system, structure, teaching etc. As a result they become over-zealous and as is the way with any kind of extreme behaviour, alienate others and lose any chance of influence they have with the wider Collective.

Another dysfunctional aspect is when they try to bring change and improvement to either an organisation or person who is not looking for it and is deeply resistant to it. If you do not want change, do not seek it and are deeply fixed and rigid in resisting it, there is nothing more annoying than someone wanting to change you. It never works - never mind that it may be needed, and Sirians need to learn to discern where their gifts can do most good and take them to the aid of those who are willing.

Another potentially dysfunctional aspect of Sirian gifts can be that their propensity for planning becomes the be all and end all. They get stuck in the planning process, going round and round, improving things each time, but never implementing. They can perfect the methodology again and again rather than implementing it.

One other potentially dysfunctional aspect can be the sense of wholeness Sirians embody. They have a very balanced energy and come from a place of wholeness within, but taken to the extreme this can isolate them as they feel so whole in their Self that they do not need or seek anyone else.

Whilst this self-reliance may be laudable at one level, it is not fulfilling any function to the Collective, nor helping to lift society as a whole to a better level of expression.

Star Family - Spica

Spica is the brightest star in the constellation of Virgo, and is also known as Alpha Virginus.

Spicans are a fairly rare Soul Family – their numbers on Earth are likely to only be in the thousands and their home planet itself does not have many Souls on it.

Their home planet is much less dense than Earth, and souls from Spica are more used to living embodied in bodies of Light than in the physical density of Earth.

Spicans love lots of space - to them, the Earth is a very crowded place. They like to spend time alone, and in nature if possible, where they have comparative energetic peace and quiet.

It is not unusual for Spicans to live alone in remote areas or to work in farming or in forestry. Their home planet gave them a lot of energetic space, and they hold the echo of this within them.

So it is important that they have plenty of space both in their homes and also maybe a bolthole in the countryside if they live in the city. There is a lot of energetic noise when lots of humanity gathers together and being able to escape can help them maintain balance and clear their energy. They can also be quite electro-sensitive so keeping at least their bedroom free of gadgets and minimising exposure to electromagnetic fields can be of benefit.

Spicans can need quiet time alone in order to remain energetically balanced. There is nothing stand offish about this – it is just that they need this time for their own health and well-being.

Spicans can struggle with the practicalities of our planet – they are used to bodies of Light not density and the practicalities it brings with it. For this reason, they may seem spacey and ungrounded at times, or even a little vague and dreamy, but they have a serenity to them that is both attractive and can be quite startling in this busy world. This serenity and clarity is a great gift to bring to Earth at this particular time of chaos.

One good strategy for Spicans to engage better with the practicalities of life can be to automate and make daily domestic stuff like paying bills easy, doing things like finding a tax accountant, a household cleaner, setting up alerts for renewals and so on. This takes care of the everyday chores, which they otherwise might overlook, efficiently.

One of the major gifts Spicans bring to Earth is the gift of non-judgment. They are very expansive, non-judgmental people, and they have the ability to see the bigger picture behind the choices others make and take a stance of neutrality towards their decisions and actions. As a result, people tend to be very honest with them as they enable others to feel a sense of safety and that they are not going to be judged.

They have a very live-and-let-live outlook on life and are loving and warm-hearted, but can sometimes come over as rather aloof and detached because their lack of judgment and neutrality can be misinterpreted.

It is not that they don't care, they do. It is just that they have no quibble with whatever floats your boat. But it can seem to some that this neutrality comes across as uncaring – nothing is further from the truth, it is just this neutrality is misinterpreted.

However, there are environments which desperately need this type of neutrality – mediation for example – and when they can bring that neutrality to the right environment that energy of neutrality is beautiful and serves a high purpose.

Spicansy are excellent at holding a very energetically clear space for others, bringing their calm neutrality to this space, enabling others to see themselves clearly from within this held space. Very useful for counselling or transformational professions where this gift can really shine, but not useful in environments where people do not WANT to see themselves clearly.

So, without realising it Spicans can find themselves triggering others – not because of anything they do, but because others might not like what they see of themselves around them. This can cause them hurt and pain and they can withdraw confused and rather bewildered about what it is they have done, unless they understand what is happening. This innate neutrality which is so much a part of them can serve others as a catalyst for transformation – and they just need to show up to do it – but not everyone wants it!

Spicans are often dreamers and visionaries, and they hold the codes for enlightenment, a state requiring a balanced aura. They hold this knowledge within them, but in human form are working their way back to it – and showing us how it is done at the same time!

The emotional and physical aspects of living in physicality can seem very dense and heavy to Spicans and they can find their own emotional body quite overwhelming. It is easy for them to get stuck in their own feelings, trying to endlessly process and analyse emotions rather than just releasing them and letting them flow through. As a result it can feel like it takes a lot of effort to get anything done.

Dysfunctional

The major dysfunctional aspect of this Soul Family can be a tendency to escapism. As I have stated, Spicans can feel like the practicalities of life are very cumbersome and overwhelming and find being in physicality very challenging. They can even come to resent being in a physical body.

This can lead to them abdicating responsibility for the everyday mundane practicalities of life, such as making money, and keeping body and soul together, telling themselves they can do without, they don't need three meals a day, comfort and warmth, nice things or whatever it may be, and end up embracing a very austere lifestyle.

As a result they can buy into the minimalist way of living - but there is a difference between being a minimalist by choice and being a minimalist because you can't afford to buy things!

Minimalism IF it is chosen is great, for those who want to experience it, but living austerely due to lack of responsibility around finances and lifestyle is not so good. Spicans need to acknowledge the difference between the two and put in place a strategy of streamlining and simplifying things to make being in physicality more palatable.

As for all of us, the physical body is a vehicle of Divine self-expression, so Spicans need to see the physical body in this light and come to value it and the experiences it can give them, as well as being aware of how physical deprivation, poor nutrition, lack of exercise etc can give some import to their mental/emotional health, and be prepared to do what is needed at this level to keep themselves healthy and balanced.

Spicans may find themselves drawn to the spiritual development world and this can be another aspect of escapism, as it gives them the chance to escape everyday life and disappear into a fantasy world. Sitting around meditating or floating around in the ether is all very well but it is avoiding the purpose of living and is a form of spiritual escapism.

Because of this desire to get away from the heaviness of 3D living they may buy into some of the more magical and unrealistic aspects of the New-Age world. In the longer term this is likely to lead to resentment building up as they come to realise that making a vision board and meditating does not actually lead to "effortless" manifestation.

As so many have found, it takes a little more work than that!

Star Family
Vega

Vega is the brightest star in the constellation of Lyra, the Harp, and also was once our North Star. Due to the wobble of Earth's axis the North Star changes over thousands of years. At the moment it is Polaris, but in about 12,000 years it will once again be Vega.

The Lyran sector of the galaxy is often referred to as the Cradle of Civilisation as it is said to be the original birthplace of all humanoid races. The planets and systems within the constellation of Lyra were beautiful and abundant and all existed in generally peaceful cooperation until the Lyran Wars, when war broke out between some of the race of this constellation whose levels of consciousness were digressing, destroying some of the planets and causing a diaspora of Lyran refugees settling other parts of the galaxy.

Vega, being somewhat distant from the main Lyran system escaped this destruction and Vegans were initially a relatively peaceful and gentle race of beings. There developed a strong polarization toward the masculine on Vega, leading to some conflict with other Lyrans who are more oriented to the Divine Feminine. However, like all the lightworker Starseeds those here on this planet follow an ethos of service to others. They are relatively rare to find incarnating here on Earth.

Vegans have a strong ego and are known for their brave and independent nature, however they can be quite introspective and focused on

Facing northeast at nightfall in mid-May

spirituality and being of service to others through the many levels of physical, emotional and energetic healing. They have a strong intellectual streak, which is usually balanced with creativity.

Despite this Vegans were technologically advanced – the two are not incompatible with spirituality, we are just having a problem sorting out an inclusive way of achieving this here on Earth. Some Vegans here are choosing to help develop these fields of knowledge on Earth and helping to demonstrate how science, technology and spirituality can all co-exist and be of service to the well-being and upliftment of all, others are working to help show us a different way of 'being' on this planet.

They are creative souls, even when working with technology and create through a much more intuitive 'knowing' sense than from an intellectual or technologically based one. They are often to be found working with new healing-based technologies and expanding our understanding of the use of metaphysical modalities such as crystals and energy healing and naturally inclining towards ways in which we can work in harmony with our planet.

Vegans have a natural magnetism and can easily become the focus of attention within a group. Energetically, when attention is focused on them, it seems to amplify their gifts of being able to inspire and touch their audience in a way which uplifts.

They have a natural reticence and are not attention seekers and do not seek the limelight but seem to come alive and thrive when circumstances contrive to thrust them into it in a way which is both charming and delightful. It is not egoic-based and if they have knowledge, information and insights which can truly be of help to humanity at this time, they should be encouraged to step up and put themselves out there, as they have much of value to share.

When they share their gifts, they help inspire others to do the same. It is a beautiful, balanced flow of energies.

This ability to hold space potentially for large groups is an innate gift which is energetically triggered when a lot of attention is directed at them. They make great teachers, for example, or group leaders or even entertainers.

To others they appear strong and capable and have a natural confidence which they themselves often don't recognise. This confidence enables them to question themselves, be open and willing to explore new ideas and try new things, although it is unlikely they will recognise this as being out of the ordinary – it is just who they are!

Vegans have a natural warmth and vivacity that it is difficult not to respond to and energetically they make us feel good, providing a natural pick-me-up just by being in their presence.

Vegans often seek variety and challenges. They are curious about everything, and seek answers. Rather than be specialists they are the original 'renaissance man' or polymaths, using that innate sense of 'feeling' what is truth and non-truth to guide their investigations and inform their inner knowing.

Many Vegans have the ability to combine creative expression with intellectual expression in a balanced way which can be both unique and extremely helpful in our polarised society. They can stand as role models for others to demonstrate a more balanced way of being.

Vegans are often not good finishers, being good at starting a new line of investigation, project, artistic creation etc, but being distracted into a new area before it is fully finished. There can be lessons in self-discipline for Vegans in carrying something through to completion, and surrounding themselves with those who encourage this.

Vegans do not respond well to restriction, needing their freedom. They love travelling, but also need time alone. Indeed they often seek their own company and are not unhappy with it.

Whilst Vegans are very responsible and caring in relationships their need for alone time, as well as their broad range of interests and their natural magnetism and caring (which can attract those demanding and needy for their attention), can leave those in intimate relationships with a Vegan feeling neglected as they can spread themselves too thinly. Healthy boundaries need to be established in this respect and Vegans need to prioritise caring for both their own needs and those close to them before that of relative strangers or acquaintances.

Vegans are natural healers, and if they chose to work within this field can be excellent therapists. They have a natural affinity for rocks and crystals and nature and may choose to incorporate these in their healing work or they may take their caring abilities into the more defined healthcare system of society as healthcare workers, physical well-being experts and coaches, mental health carers, teachers, or even social workers. This is not necessarily a good thing if they become part of a large corporate-type body as the system can crush their need for freedom and lack of restriction leaving them drained and exhausted.

Dysfunctional

When Vegans allow others with unhealthy boundaries who are needy and co-dependent to monopolise their time and attention they can start to tip into dysfunction. Whilst it can be flattering to have someone hanging on your every word, looking at you adoringly and treating you like the centre of their universe, it can demand inappropriate levels of attention and support.

This is most often seen in those Vegans whose natural magnetism and gifts attracts a bunch of hangers-on which they then fail to discern are energy drains who are taking advantage of them. They can feel overly responsible for these people and their well-being.

Healthy boundaries and a level of insight as to the level of neediness and integrity of others can help these loving and giving souls to be more balanced in promoting an equal and even exchange of energy that is more appropriate.

Another potential dysfunctional aspect can be that they feel overly responsible for the care and well-being of others, neglecting both what is best for themselves and for their loved ones. There can be a need to understand that we all have to accept responsibility for the choices we make and the actions we take. Self-responsibility is one of the things each soul has to learn, so some tough love can help a soul grown and over-nurturing and over-caring can be inappropriate.

Final Word

Probably the question I get asked most is 'Where does this information come?' and much as I would like to point people towards certain sources there is no really straightforward answer I can give.

For me, it has been a process which has taken many years to understand and come into a position to compile coherent information. Some of this information I flirted with for many years, but did not really fully understand it let alone know what to do with it. I began searching what seems like a long time ago now for answers to questions I couldn't even begin to verbalise at that time. I was seeking, and trying to follow, a thread of energy that led I knew not where. I read books, studied courses and texts, booked into expensive workshops and searched ancient teachings for years.

I kept knocking up against something that if I am honest, I wasn't quite ready to explore. It took me from the 'woo-woo' and New Age category into the definitely weird and way out and my conservative conditioning – already stretched to breaking point – wasn't ready for the next step.

Occasionally I would find information that I knew with a deep energetic knowing in my cell tissue was solid, it rang with the vibration of Truth for me. And I knew so much of what I had picked up from books/courses/teachers was hollow of that vibration, or had glimpses of it within the work, but was lacking something.

So I was constantly following the odd thread that had the right resonance and kept ending up at the same point. There comes a time you have to leap off the cliff. So I went weird, I went way out, I went cosmic .....and I started to fly.

Mad as it was I started to find a narrative and understanding that finally began to make sense and gave me the answers I was seeking.

I came to understand that much of this information is held within the consciousness grids and morphogenetic fields of the planet, within the Akashic, as well as within my own cell tissue. And for many years – since I began searching in fact – I had been getting energetic 'downloads' that I felt like electrical storms in my body.

For over 10 years I didn't understand, nor could anyone explain the process that was happening. My default to it was instinctively to resist the incoming energy, resulting in frequent and debilitating 3 day headaches which unfolded through a process where my head felt as if it were caught in an electrical net that left me feeling beached every time.

They were happening every two weeks or so at one point and it was only when a visit to a therapist who had been trained in a certain energetic 'seeing' technique coincided with one of these episodes that I started to get the understanding I needed and work with the process little by little until the headaches stopped.

So these packets of energy information are now downloading into my field at regular intervals. When I find the right 'key' it unlocks. Sometime it is waking in the middle of the night and 'poof' all of a sudden I understand something or some concept, almost like it arrives fully formed. I can then do research to fill in some of the details. Or maybe I read a sentence or hear a phrase and like a blossom opening inside me a whole understanding unfolds, or I may find, when I turn to a certain area of research I haven't covered before as soon as I bring it into focus information is just sitting there waiting for me to turn my attention its way.

And then there is the process of synchronicity with books that are helpful popping up on the internet, or being shown to me by friends, or an internet page appearing I didn't know I needed.

All of this research process helps me fill in any gaps I have. There is plenty of information out there in various forms, it turns out, it is just lost in the sea of noise that is the disinformation and deflection agenda that is being worked so skilfully by the Other Side – and believe me, there is an Other Side, Dark Forces, Fallen Angelics, Intruder Races, Shadow Agendas, whatever you want to call it, that is working hard to keep this information from you, and label it conspiracy, nonsense, fantasy and so on wherever it can.

It is up to us – you and me – to not be fooled and to hone our own inner discernment as to what expands and empowers us, and what disempowers and keeps us in a lesser and impoverished state of being.

There are also records called the CDT Plates – I've included information about them in Appendix D – and there is a lot of information from these to be found if you search, some of it very dodgy to be sure, as it has been deliberately mangled by the likes of the so-called Egyptian god Thoth who managed to get his hands of a couple at one stage, but there is other information, other sources which is rock solid. But you have to look for it, and you have to be discerning as to sources. There are several people who, since the start of the millennium have been tasked with transcribing and teaching some of the CDT information. It is there to be found, but it is like an energetic treasure trail you have to follow to get to it.

It is not mainstream – mainstream, so-called New Age is hijacked on the whole – and once I had found my way past all the diversions and blocks to getting at this information stuff has been unlocking thick and fast in the last few years – I read a sentence often and it 'unpacks' all the information downloaded inside me at some previous point.

I find it extraordinary, if I am frank, and it has been a learning process to trust it all.

My purpose now is to start putting together a 'narrative' thread others can follow easily as so much available can be very dense to penetrate. It feels to me the time is right to begin to make this information – carefully guarded for millennia – more widely available.

So that is what I am starting to do, beginning with this book. Energetically the environment is beginning to support this. There is more, much more, to come, when the timing is right.

I hope you find this useful and informative. Please remember I offer this as my current understanding of a very complex topic, which is re-revealing itself in layers, and I present all the information here to you from the intent and desire to help other Starseeds in the awakening process to come back into full remembrance more quickly.

After all, we need every one to remember why they are here and what they can do to help heal both the Planet and the Collective.

But always, always trust your own inner Gnosis. If anything you have read does not resonate with your own Truth, or you are not ready to go down this particular route just yet, let it go as you would leaves on the wind and continue to seek your particular Truth or route towards the new realities you are learning about.

I fully understand that my Truth may not be your Truth, and that is okay, because we are all looking at this amazing cosmos from different directions and different levels, so we will all have different perspectives.

Wishing you joy and love on your journey

Saira xxx

Appendices

Appendix A
The Emerald Covenant

The Emerald Covenant is a promise made by God/Source/Universal Consciousness to all beings in this Fallen Universe that every Soul would be eventually found and returned back to their original spiritual home according to the Divine plan of Ascension.

It is overseen by the Guardian Alliance, founded by the great beings of the fields of consciousness at the highest levels of frequency of this Time Matrix or Universe, known as the Breneau, specifically the Emerald Order Breneau, hence the term Emerald Covenant.

This is the original 'Creation Contract' and in response to this Emerald Order Breneau Founders incarnate into specific race lineages in order to take on form, by stepping down their frequency of consciousness into bodies which hold high frequency templating, specifically the Lyran-Sirian lineages that originate from Sirius B called the Azurites and the Oraphim.

This enables them to oversee the lower density worlds and help direct missions such as that which is underway here on Earth - the 'rescue' of Angelic humanity from the outside interference and control that has been imposed on it, taking away its free will evolution, progression and spiritual freedom.

It upholds the Law of One and from the Earth perspective seeks to heal the genetic templating and DNA damage inflicted on the Angelic lineages, as well as rehabilitating the Fallen Races. Many of these beings are here on Earth at this time in the guise of what are called Indigos.

The Law of One is a way of Love and therefore force is not met with force, but with loving kindness, negotiation and compassion in order to help heal the planet and support the liberation of this planet. Bringing in higher frequencies and holding them here in the Earth grids not only helps the consciousness of all beings connected to those grids, but makes it more and more uncomfortable for low frequency beings here on the planet as they find this hard to tolerate. They then have a choice – to match their frequency to that prevailing, or leave.

As part of this strategy a pathway of disclosure is being followed helping to make amnesic humanity aware once more of its origins, and true galactic history and its purpose here on the planet. It is not the first time this has been done – each time the Fallen Races quickly intervene and confuse, muddle, re-write, denigrate or simply hide what has been brought through. It is hoped this time that along with the rising frequencies and Stellar Activation Cycle sufficient number will 'wake up' to the extend it will make a Collective difference.

If sufficient critical mass can be stimulated to activate enough frequency within their DNA templating not only can the consciousness grids of the planet and the Stargates, which have been badly damaged and hijacked, be corrected back to their original blueprint, but the Angelic human DNA potential can become fully realised once more, activating their 12-strand (and beyond) template, and humanity can then take their place here on Earth as Guardians of the Planetary grids and Stargates, as well as taking their place as members of the Interdimensional Free World Councils (IFWC).

At the heart of the Emerald Covenant sits the Law of One, and the reverence for all Life, upholding the right of races and beings to choose and live the path of unity should they wish without interference or fear.

Appendix B
The Law of One

The Law of One recognises the Universal Truth that All is One – a truth that still echoes through many of our ancient spiritual teachings, and is recognised as Unity Consciousness. It contains within it the awareness that we all come from the same Source and are all part of this Source. No matter our shape, size, colour, point of origin etc, every living entity is connected and part of the whole due to this simple fact.

When properly recognised and understood this is a very powerful and unifying force. Love, the frequency of Love is the organic consciousness of God/Source/Creator or whatever word you wish to use. Love pervades all Creation, all beings, and unites us all. We simply have to recognise this and work to embody this.

Each being who is committed to the Law of One seeks to embody this unity principle, to practice loving kindness and compassion and embody the understanding that what you do to one, ultimately you do to all, including oneself.

It seeks to recognise that each being, each spark of consciousness that is the Divine incarnate, is on its own journey of experience, is evolving along its own path. Each soul evolves in its own time and all are at different levels, but that is ok and as it should be. Each will follow different timelines and participate in different holographic realities, and that too is as it should be.

All have value, all are interconnected and all are interdependent. By living in awareness of this understanding, by living in such a way that expresses unconditional Love to all Creation, it brings us into a state of unity with Source/Universal Consciousness (again use the word which means most to you).

By adhering to these very simple principles it can bring us into a high state of expanded consciousness and frequency that unifies and leads us to spiritual freedom.

The Law of One has been the founding principle of this God World or Time Matrix since it was created around 950 billion years ago. It is a unifying principle for all races across the galaxy, excepting those Fallen Races whose templating digressed to the extent they chose to detach from these unifying principles in order to follow their own agendas of aggression, domination, control and destruction.

The Law of One was gifted to humanity at its original seeding here on Earth via what are called the Emerald Founder Records or the Cloister Dora-Teura (CDT) Holographic Plates. These plates contain not only the teachings of the Law of One, but also the knowledge of the origins, genetics and purpose of the human race, and included also the galactic history of this Time Matrix which is the birthright of all Angelic humans. There are 12 plates in all and they were closely guarded and protected. As you can imagine they are highly prized by both Angelic and Fallen races alike.

Practices

There are seven simple practices that make up the Law of One:

The Practice of Unity Consciousness – encapsulated in the saying All is One and embracing the Divine in everything. This is not a question of all *becoming* one (like a hive mind), but rather of Unity in Diversity, acknowledging our common Divinity whilst celebrating our individual uniqueness.

The Practice of Loving Yourself - we cannot truly love others if we do not love ourselves. By loving, honouring and respecting oneself we are acknowledging the Divine with us and embodying the Divine energy of Love within us. It is an act of Self Sovereignty.

The Practice of Loving Others – by learning to love ourselves, we learn to love others and see within them the same Divine energy which is within us. Hold others in the same love, respect and honour that you hold yourself, and have compassion and non-judgment for all, for we are all on unique paths and all are of equal value.

The Practice of Loving Earth and Nature – Divine Consciousness is alive within all things. Our Mother Earth and all her creations, all her kingdoms of plants, animals, minerals and all the unseen kingdoms of nature spirits, all are part of the Divine and all contain Divine consciousness to be held in Love, respect and honour. This brings harmony to the way in which we co-exist with our close neighbours and the planet.

The Practice of Service to Others – find ways in which you can help serve others individually and also the Collective. This is not a case of overstepping personal boundaries, nor is it about egoic entitlement or attachment. It is a quiet, humble practice without expectation that is part of a flow of energy exchange which expands and extends the field of consciousness.

The Practice of Consciousness Expansion – this is a process of consciousness embodiment and recognition of the spiritual identity. If the ego still has any kind of authority it will block this from happening, and it requires discipline and awareness of the mind and thoughts and the ability to sit in patience and wait for the mind to quiet in order to listen to inner spirit and guidance. This in turn will lead you where you need to go to expand your awareness and consciousness into a gnosis of the sovereignty and unity of all things free from fear and dogma.

The Practice of Responsible Co-Creatorship – as our consciousness expands and activates ever greater levels of our DNA templating we become more aware of our Divine purpose of being a co-creator with God. We share a unity of purpose and direction and seek to live in a way which totally embodies this. Nothing is done from ego, but from the gnosis, or inner knowing, of unity consciousness and that we do not control, possess or know better than anything or anyone else. We therefore do not impose our will, but seek to express the Divine energy of Love which flows through us to all Creation.

Remember also that there are many paths that lead back to God/Source/Creator. None are better than any other, all have equal value, and each being's journey is unique. All comes from God/Source/Creator and all should be used to honour and serve the Divine in Creation.

It is also worth noting that your spiritual practice should feel right for you – it should be your own, not imposed on you, so do not let others tell you what the form and structure should be, where and when you should do it and what you should do - leave aside anything that does not feel right for you at this time, and in this place, and follow your inner Divine authority.

By putting our focus on Other rather than Self we expand our awareness and therefore our spiritual power and effectiveness out into the world.

Appendix C
The Guardian Alliance

The Guardian Alliance (GA) was created 568 million years ago by the Elohim of the Emerald Order Breneau of Harmonic Universe or Density 5 of this Time Matrix after what is called the Angelic Wars, otherwise known as the Lyran Wars.

They are a smaller, specialised group within a greater Guardian organisation called the Interdimensional Association of Free Worlds (IAFW). Membership of the GA spans all the matter frequencies and dimensions across time-space.

There are an enormous number of co-operative organisations within the Guardian Alliance (GA) from many different interstellar, multi-dimensional and inter-time species who all work together under the auspices of the Law of One to help with the development and evolution of cultures and races across the many multi-dimensional levels of this Universe.

One of the primary purposes of the GA is to assist the Founders Races to protect, guide and oversee the creation and evolution of the Oraphim-Turaneusiam Guardian Angelic Christos human lineage and assist in its peaceful and harmonious integration and evolution into the interdimensional Guardian Angelic communities.

There are various galactic, inter-dimensional and extra-dimensional races which do not wish the Christos races well and seek their destruction and thus the Guardian Alliance task force was founded to protect all races of this lineage from the intended devastation.

They are tasked with protecting and insuring that the individual races and species are able to each discover and fulfil their genetic plan to their full potential as was intended, and to increase levels of security in this Time Matrix to allow this to unfold.

They serve as the governing body for over 10 million 'Law of One' Star League Nations within Densities 1 – 4 of our Universe.

The Guardian Alliance also serves as the administrative body for the 12 GA Signet Councils each of which are one of the Primary Guardians of the 12 Universal Star Gates which make up the Universal Templar Complex of this Time Matrix or Universe.

Appendix D
The CDT Plates or Founder Records

The CDT Plates or Cloister-Dora-Teura Plates are 12 holographic recording, storage and transmission devices gifted to the human race lineage by the Founders Races and contain the full evolutionary history of life within our Time Matrix from 950 billion years ago to the present, as well as extensive educational teachings around Creation Mechanics and advanced Spiritual Teachings.

The Plates were originally manufactured at the Founder's instigation by the 5th dimensional Taran Priests of Ur and the Maharaji Sirian-Blue Human Holy Grail Line races of the Council of Azurline.

246,000 BC they were gifted to the Urtite Human Races by the Azurite Races of Sirius B at the first seeding of physical humanity on 3-D Earth in honour of the Urtites entering the Founders Races Emerald Covenant Co-Evolution Agreement.

The CDT Plates hold the ancient records on 12 silver-metallic discs manufactured from a form of striated-selenite-quartz crystal which is organic to the HU2 or 2nd Density planet of Sirius B, surrounding a radioactive isotopic core. This is then overlaid or encased in a hybrid-metal silver-alloy compound which is organic to Earth.

On the gifting of these plates to Urtite Humanity the first written translation was undertaken and became a collection of large books called the Maharata. This was a collection of over 500,000 pages of text transcription held in 590 large embossed leather-bound volumes written on a form of durable textile-paper resembling crisp, semi-translucent vellum.

The original transcription was in the Anuhazi language, the first spoken and written language of this Time Matrix.

The 12 CDT Plates were kept on Earth until the Urtite human culture was wiped out in 208,216 BC at the time of a failed Stellar Activation Cycle, when there was a deliberate pole shift achieved through machinations and infiltration of Negative Forces wanting to take down the human lineage.

Just prior to this the Sirius B Azurite races retrieved 10 of the 12 CDT Plates and placed them under the protection of the Azurite Universal Templar Security Team.

The CDT Plates are highly coveted by all interstellar races because of the information they contain. But there is also a secondary reason why they are so highly prized. They are part of a large apparatus that includes 12 further silver discs, which are larger than the CDT Plates, called the 12 Signet Shields. Signet refers to Stargate and they are a technology through which the 12 Primary Star Gates of the Universal Templar Complex of this Time Matrix, spanning the densities and dimensions, can be activated.

Between them the 12 CDT Plates can be used to remotely manually activate the Signet Shields and their corresponding Stargates. As Activators of the Signet Shields, in the wrong hands ownership of the CDT Plates could be devastating.

Whilst the Azurites reclaimed 10 of the 12 CDT Plates, 2 of them, and all 12 of the Signet Shields were lost, moving between various competing human and Fallen Angelic Legions on Earth since this time.

In the 1600s the Azurites finally regained possession of one of the missing plates, and in November 1999 the last of them, called the 'Tables of Testimony' by the Knights Templar, was retrieved.

The 12 Signet Shields are currently buried in various secret locations around the Earth.

Since 208,216 BC the Azurites have offered the human race at specific points in the timeline dispensations of knowledge translated from the CDT Plates.

We see these crop up at various times in our history only for the pure teachings to be very quickly – and deliberately – compromised, corrupted, distorted and misrepresented. The Book of Enoch is a case in point, as are the teachings of the Essenes known as John the Baptist and Jesus Christ. The Cathars also held information through genuine Essene records but were exterminated by the Vatican in 1244 AD. Hindu, Chinese, Tibetan, African, Egyptian, Mayan, Incan and Celtic-Druidic lines have all brought through information at various points in these culture's history, only for it all to suffer the same fate of destruction or distortion by the Negative Forces.

Translations of CDT Plates have been returning to humanity through the auspices of certain individuals at this time of Stellar Activation Cycle in order to help guide humanity through the process, and helping restore the lost knowledge and understanding of humanity's lineage and purpose to the badly manipulated and mind-controlled population of Earth.[11]

So what information do the CDT Plates contain? Different discs contain certain types of information which when brought together as a whole form a complete Sacred Science.

Amongst the practical physical and spiritual evolutionary advancement teachings is the full evolutionary history of the development of life in our Time Matrix, extensive educational records pertaining to Founders Race Creation Mechanics, Universal Unified Field Physics, Law of One – Inner Christ teachings and Ascension-Merkaba training, the history and details of the Emerald Covenant and humanity's historical relationship to this,

---

[11] Please be aware these are not 'channelled' teaching which are often highly suspect. The CDT Plates are holographic in nature and deliver 'downloads' of frequency information which then needs to be 'translated' from its holographic, audio, visual or digital data form by the chosen individuals into our often inadequate languages.

teachings of Planetary, Galactic and Universal Star Gate mechanics, DNA Template Bio-Regenesis and Kathara Core Template Healing technologies and much more besides.

All of these were gifted to the human race in order to enable Angelic Humanity to fulfil its original 'Creation Commission' as guardians and keepers of the Universal Templar Complex – a purpose we are a long way from currently achieving at the moment.

Amongst the various books which I am aware of are:

The Book of the Dragon
The Book of Amenti
The Angelic Rosters
Keylontic Morphogenetic Science
Books of Maps and Key
The Books of Enoch

Emerald Tablets of Thoth the Atlantean

I think it is worth mentioning here what are known as the Emerald Tablets, written by Thoth the Atlantean. These are writings which are said to have formed the basis of Hermeticism, amongst other sacred teachings, given by the Egyptian/Atlantean god Thoth, also known as Hermes or Hermes Trismegistus.

Thoth is from the fallen Sirian-Anunnaki lineage. For many thousands of years he voluntarily took part in the Bio-Regenesis programme, which seeks to correct DNA distortions and return the DNA potential of anyone willing to participate to its full 12-strand potential, even those of Anunnaki origin who willingly disconnected their 12th strand.

Things had gone well, and Thoth had worked himself into such a place of trust with those running the Bio-Regenesis programmes that he had been granted a certain amount of access to the CDT plates.

In a betrayal which has echoed down the recent historical timelines, so horrific were its effects, he turned on the Guardian Alliance, stole CDT Plate 10 and instigated what is called the Eieyani Massacre, one of the more horrific of the Fallen Angelic betrayals.

He wrote the Emerald Tablets as a distorted version of the pure teachings, which have been creating havoc within mystery schools and sacred societies ever since, designed to ensure that well-meaning people were corrupted into enacting fallen, reversal ascension mechanics and having their light siphoned into the dark agendas of the Fallen Races.

So whilst the Emerald Tablets are based on CDT plate 10, they are NOT the pure teachings but a highly corrupted and damaging version.

Acknowledgements:

My thanks to the many teachers, mentors, clients and groups who over the years have helped me understand and hone my access to the information found here. It has been a puzzle put together piece by piece, through many shared conversations, meditations, insights, readings and aha moments.

And there is always more to come......

Printed in Great Britain
by Amazon